A Liar and a Killer : The True Story of Sarah Dutra

Tina Fox

Published by Trellis Publishing, 2021.

While every precaution has been taken in the preparation of this book, the publisher assumes no responsibility for errors or omissions, or for damages resulting from the use of the information contained herein.

A LIAR AND A KILLER : THE TRUE STORY OF SARAH DUTRA

First edition. July 8, 2021.

Copyright © 2021 Tina Fox.

ISBN: 979-8224793112

Written by Tina Fox.

A LIAR AND A KILLER

THE TRUE STORY OF SARAH DUTRA

2

TINA FOX

When Sarah Dutra met Elisa McNabney, she had no idea she was embarking on a friendship that would ultimately change her life – and eventually come to an end with Sarah behind bars.

"She lays on the charm."

The two women worked together at a law office owned by Elisa's husband, Larry. Elisa had met Larry in 1995, when she first applied for a position at a firm he'd owned in Las Vegas. He was a courtroom star, having defended the perpetrators of two of Nevada's most infamous crimes – a 1982 bombing extortion scheme at Harvey's casino, and a 1989 drug conspiracy trial that lasted for 13 months.

He was recognized for his quirky, fun television commercials, which depicted him riding a horse through the Nevada desert. But despite all his charm, Larry had been married five times – he was a barely-functioning alcoholic and struggled with maintaining relationships.

"He's a brilliant attorney and a natural-born leader," said Nevada District Judge Peter Breen. "He has risen several times from falls with alcohol – he always came back stronger."

After being hired as his office manager, Elisa got to work settling large cases – but just a few months later, the Nevada State Bar conducted an investigation into Larry's business, and discovered Elisa had embezzled more than $74,000 from Larry's clients.

Although Larry was forced to close his Las Vegas office, he still married Elisa in 1996, and the couple moved to Sacramento, California. According to Larry's daughter, Tavia Williams, her father "was attracted to (Elisa) because of her age and the fact that she lays on the charm." Elisa got Larry interested in the world of showing quarterhorses, which quickly became a passion more than a hobby.

In early 2000, Sarah Dutra was a 21-year old art student, studying at California State University. She responded to a newspaper ad seeking a part-time legal secretary for a wage of $3,000 per month – more than enough to help her cover her tuition. Elisa and Sarah became quite close as they worked together at Larry's office, and investigators allege that Sarah was also drawn in by the glitz and glamour of the horse shows Elisa and Larry regularly brought her to.

Debbie Kail, a horse trainer who had worked closely with the McNabneys, testified that in the weeks before Larry vanished, she had several uncomfortable encounters with Elisa and Sarah. According to Debbie, Elisa would often brag to friends that she would "make sure Larry has enough to drink" so that she could go out and party with her friends without him. She also claimed to have spiked his wine with painkillers.

"She had told me previously that she had gotten Vicodin and she had put that in Larry's wine ... just to see what would happen," Debbie testified. "She said it didn't even drop him."

According to statements provided by witnesses and other documentation, Larry McNabney was struggling – his law practice was suffering, and he'd started drinking heavily. And he'd apparently also begun to worry about his wife – police stated that he is said to have told a friend that "if anything happens to me, tell the cops Elisa did it."

A dangerous relationship

The last time Larry McNabney was seen alive was at a horse show on September 10, 2001, with his wife Elisa and their friend, Sarah Dutra. In the statement she gave detectives, Sarah said she'd left the show early, but had then returned after hearing from Elisa that Larry wasn't feeling well.

After renting a wheelchair to move Larry from his truck into their Los Angeles hotel, prosecutors allege that the two women concocted a murderous scheme– to poison Elisa's husband and steal money from his practice. In the hotel room, prosecutors claim, they proceeded to inject him with a drug called acepromazine – a horse tranquilizer.

Elisa had just been asking about horse tranquilizers a few days earlier, Debbie Kail told a packed courtroom when the case was brought to trial. She had asked Debbie if a certain horse tranquilizer could kill a person – and Debbie had told her that it could. Elisa knew that Debbie carried a veterinary kit containing a variety of drugs for horses, including some tranquilizers. Although Debbie said she kept the drugs locked up, Elisa knew the combination to access the kid.

According to what Elisa told police, the women then took her unconscious husband out to Yosemite National Park, with the intent to bury his body when they got there. However, the sandy desert ground was extremely hard, and Larry was still alive.

"He wanted to sleep," read Elisa's statement to police. "His face was droopy."

Sarah maintains that she refused to help bury Larry in the Nevada desert – so, without any ideas for a backup plan, the women stuffed Larry's body into the refrigerator in the couple's garage after he died when they got back home.

"I think this community, our family, and his friends really lost a great person," said Larry's daughter, Tavia, just months after her father's body was found. "He was a very honourable man. He had such a way with people, we just miss him. This was our first Father's Day without him, and there's not something to fill that void."

Sarah told detectives that Elisa had threatened her – if she didn't help Elisa stuff the body into the refrigerator, she said, Elisa would have killed her. Sarah also admitted to detectives that she had travelled with Elisa after the murder had been committed – including a trip to Las Vegas when Larry's body had been stuffed in the truck of Elisa's car.

According to Elisa's daughter, 18 year old Haylei Jordan, Sarah hadn't ever appeared to be afraid of her mother. In fact, Haylei testified, she allowed Elisa to use her name on more than one occasion to make purchases that generally demand identification, like cars. Debbie Kail also testified that the relationship between Sarah and Elisa had evolved over the time she'd seen them together – to the point, she said, where it had begun to infringe on the relationship between Elisa and her husband.

"It just seemed like when Sarah would fly in and arrive, (Sarah and Elisa) would get into their little mode, and Larry would be the odd man out," she said.

Debbie's father, horse-ranch owner Greg Whalen, also testified that Larry had become increasingly uncomfortable with Sarah's constant presence in Elisa's life. According to Greg's testimony, he'd attended the horse show with the trio the weekend that Larry was poisoned, along with his daughter Debbie.

As the group had dinner together just two days before authorities claim Larry died, Greg said Larry was drinking heavily – and the more intoxicated he became, the more foul the looks and language exchanged between he and Sarah grew.

"Larry did not like Sarah," Greg told the court. "Sometimes guys talk, and he just thought that Sarah and Elisa were too close."

Greg said Larry continued to appear "disoriented and confused" throughout the weekend. According to Greg, Larry "just seemed like he wasn't himself."

"Larry was very articulate and on top of things, usually," he said. "He seemed a little depressed."

He received a call from Larry the night authorities say he died – and according to Greg, he "didn't sound so good." The next morning, Elisa and Sarah went to his hotel room to tell him that Larry was gone. According to the women, he'd left in the early morning hours.

Later that same morning, Debbie testified that she saw the two women driving away from the stables in Larry's truck. Inside the truck bed were two new shovels, bags of dirty clothes, and a wheelchair.

"I'm the one you're looking for."

Months later, according to Elisa's confession, she moved the body to a winery nearby in San Joaquin County, where it stayed until it was discovered by farm workers on February 5, 2002. Elisa had already liquidated her husband's assets – including his truck and a diamond ring – for a total of more than $500,000, and vanished in a brand new red Jaguar – but not before cashing plenty of settlement checks awarded to victims of personal injury, and making up a number of excuses to explain away Larry's continued absence from both work and the horse shows they attended regularly.

"(Elisa) was keeping appearances up like she was still running the firm," Nelida Stone, a spokeswoman for the San Joaquin County Sheriff's Department, said at a press conference. "All this time, she was still taking everybody's money."

Sometimes, they used fairly simple cover stories, like that Larry was unavailable at the time of the call, or that he was out of town for a court appearance. But as time went on, the excuses become more and more elaborate – his absence was attributed to a stint in rehab, a move to Costa Rica, or even that he was living with a cult.

Friends told investigators that after Larry stopped coming with them to the horse shows, Elisa's appearance also changed quite drastically. She lightened her already light brown hair, started dressing in younger, more stylish clothes, and dropped about 30 pounds between September and late November.

"She and her friend Sarah Dutra now looked a lot alike, even sounded alike," read a quote from a horse show friend in an affidavit for a search warrant.

Larry McNabney, shockingly, hadn't even been reported missing until the end of November – months after he'd first been poisoned after the horse show. The report was filed November 30 by a newly hired employee at Larry's law firm. Although she'd been hired by Elisa, the employee had started to become suspicious that her boss never came in to work, and she had noticed that Elisa and Sarah frequently made misleading statements about his potential whereabouts.

Another missing persons report was filed in January, a few days before Elisa fled California. This time, the report was filed by Larry's own son, which attracted the attention of Sacramento police – but when they went to interview Elisa, she was already gone.

Despite making her getaway, Elisa wasn't able to enjoy her freedom for long. A nationwide manhunt was launched after Larry's body was found, and Elisa hadn't left the country. She was living in Destin, Florida, and using the alias of Shane Ivaroni. On March 14, she went to dinner and a movie with 48 year old, recently divorced Destin man named Robert Murphy. The pair had attended a Kid Rock concert just a week earlier, and after seeing a movie, she spent the night at his home.

The next morning, he discovered that his date had stolen $600 in cash – along with his pickup truck. However, he also found a note, promising that she would return in a few days. She'd also left the keys to her Jaguar, which he then drove to work. The police were not far behind.

After talking to Robert, the police set up a stake out at his home in an attempt to locate Elisa. They found her soon after, relaxing by the swimming pool at a condominium complex near the house. Her hair, which had been long and light brown when she was married to Larry, was now short and jet black. And while she'd worn a size 10 when Larry was alive, she'd managed to get herself down to a size 3. She was almost unrecognizable.

"She said, 'I'm the one you're looking for,'" said Cpl. Rick Hord with the Okaloosa County Sheriff's Department. "She was tired of running. We got lucky – she was ready to talk."

Booked into Hernando County Jail, Elisa confessed to law enforcement while awaiting extradition back to California – a hand-written, three page admission of guilt.

"This admission may be the only time she has told the truth in years," said San Joaquin County deputy district attorney Lester Fleming. "This investigation involved separating the facts from the fiction."

But just one week later, on Easter Sunday, Elisa took matters into her own hands and hanged herself right in her jail cell. In her suicide note, she asked her lawyer to sue the jail for failing to prevent the suicide, requesting that any funds received as a result of the lawsuit be passed on to her children.

"This is all I can give to my children... my actions now will allow them to move into the future without this heavy burden," she wrote in the note. "They won't have to watch my trial on Court TV. It should all die with me."

A cold-blooded move

She was wrong, though. She'd told police that her friend, Sarah Dutra, was her "partner in crime." Sarah was also charged with Larry's murder, and went on trial in 2003. If convicted of first-degree murder, she faced the possibility of life imprisonment with no chance of parole – particularly since the charges included the special circumstances allegation of "murder for financial gain."

While the initial charge was for capital murder, a jury found Sarah guilty instead of voluntary manslaughter and being an accessory to murder.

"She is a murderer," said prosecutor Thomas Testa, requesting that Sarah be handed the maximum sentence. "She should have been convicted of murder, but unfortunately, we have to respect the jury's verdict. I implore the court, do justice in this case. Throw the book at Sarah Dutra."

Sarah's attorney, Kevin Clymo, pointed out that before she met Elisa, Sarah Dutra was an honours student at Vacaville High School with no prior history of criminal activity.

"I would ask the court in this case, your honour, to grant probation for Miss Dutra," he said, pleading for leniency.

Sarah's mother Karen also testified on her daughter's behalf, demonstrating to the court that despite her involvement in Larry McNabney's murder, Sarah had a "tender side." According to Karen, Sarah spent much of her time in prison tending to other inmates suffering from illnesses including breast cancer and heart conditions.

Karen, who visited her daughter every week at the Chowchilla prison, said Sarah was honing her art skills from behind bars, as well – even bringing some of Sarah's completed works with her to the stand.

"Prison is something I think you have to get used to," she said. "Sarah had to learn to defend herself, stand up to others, too."

The family also wrote a letter to Garber on Sarah's behalf, detailing her youth, success in academics, and her potential future in the world of art.

"From a young age, Sarah has reached out to those less fortunate (than) herself with an accepting nature, looking only for the 'good' in others," the letter read. "This past year has been a nightmare for our entire family. With Sarah's promising future, it has been difficult to fathom the situation with which she found herself entangled. We love our daughter and struggle to accept the fact that Sarah has been found guilty."

Another letter, from Sarah's close friend and former roommate Jennifer Murray, attested to Sarah's clean past and caring nature.

"Anyone that truly knew her would describe her as a friend of integrity that would always go out of her way to help," she wrote. "Although I do not dispute Sarah's involvement with Mr. McNabney's demise, I do truly believe she had been manipulated into her role."

However, Judge Bernard Garber determined that Sarah showed "little remorse" for her role in the death of Larry McNabney, and imposed the maximum sentence of eleven years, eight months. According to Garber, Sarah's "sociopathic personality" and "chilling" descriptions of the grisly murder made him refuse the possibility of probation or a reduced sentence.

"The defendant, along with (Elisa), drags the victim's body down the stairs in the Woodbridge house, stuffs him into the refrigerator ... (and) duct tapes the refrigerator door shut," he said. "And then, they leave him in that refrigerator for about three months or so."

Then, he added, Sarah invited McNabney's son, Joe, out to the house for an evening of partying – while his father's dead body was crammed inside of the taped up refrigerator. According to Larry McNabney's daughter Tavia Williams, this was a "cold-blooded" move – and Garber agreed.

"If that's not callousness, I don't know what is," he said. "Probation is denied."

Testa was pleased, and apologized to the victim's family for Sarah choosing not to address them in court.

"How she has torn apart our family and our hearts ... what she has put us through over the last few months has been horrific," said Tavia.

"Every day we sat in court, you would smile and wave at your dad, showing no respect or remorse ... for this unthinkable act. Even while they showed pictures of our dad with body parts sticking out of the ground, or the (video) tapes would describe what the two of you did to our dad, there was never evidence by your body language that you were ever sorry."

Sarah was also ordered by the court to pay restitution in the amount of $157,000 to some of Larry's clients, as well as the attorney fees for her own representation.

A series of unsuccessful appeals followed the initial trial. According to appellate justices, the trial judge who had presided over Sarah's case had "overstepped his bounds" by sentencing her to the maximum eleven years – the standard term for voluntary manslaughter was just six years.

Sarah had served eighty-five per cent of that sentence when she was finally released from the Central California Women's Facility on August 26, 2011.

"A parole transfer was approved from Sacramento County to Solano County, in order that she be able to maintain strong family ties to aid in her successful reintegration," said Luis Patino upon Sarah's release, speaking on behalf of the California Department of Corrections and Rehabilitation.

Sarah had a clean record prior to her involvement in the murder, and according to San Joaquin County Deputy Public Defender Keith Arthur, she only went along with Elisa's suggestions because she wanted to please her friend. According to Arthur, Sarah was also a victim – "a baby: who had been unwittingly manipulated by an older, more experienced woman, a "black widow."

"She is a secondary victim of one of the most evil people this court will ever see," Arthur said, describing to the court how Sarah had been conned into committing the crime. "She was a coward, and because of that, Larry died."

Elisa was not the real name of the friend Sarah had made at the law office. Larry had married a woman named Laren Sims, who had served time at a Florida prison – on charges of fraud and identity theft – before violating her probation, cutting her ankle monitor, and fleeding to Las Vegas with her young daughter. Throughout her life, Elisa used a total of 38 different aliases and had amassed a criminal record spanning 113 pages.

"No one can say there was a gun held to her head," said Testa, reminding the court that once Larry was dead, the women lived an extravagant lifestyle funded entirely by the money they stole from his law firm.

"Struggling toward the light"

At a resentencing in 2007, Judge F. Clark Sueyres said Sarah's own actions showed "unparalleled callousness." She seemed to have a dual personality, the judge said, noting that she was characterized both as a caring, loving artistic woman – and as a calculating killer.

"I just suggest that somehow you … reconcile these two parts of you, which we know exist, so that you can truly live the better side of yourself for your future," Sueyres said.

The 2007 resentencing was necessary after the state's 3rd District Court of Appeal overturned the 2003 sentence of Superior Court Judge Bernard Garber, who oversaw the original trial. According to the district court's ruling, the judge had "overstepped his authority."

This gave Suyres the authority to decide if Sarah should indeed serve the maximum term she had initially been sentenced, eleven years. Based on the time Sarah had already served, a shorter sentence might have meant that she could have walked free. However, Sueyres made the decision that Sarah needed to go back to prison to serve out the remainder of her original sentence.

During her time behind bars, Sarah Dutra continued to pursue her lifelong love of art. Prior to her involvement with Elisa McNabney – or Laren Sims – Sarah had studied abroad in Florence, Italy at an exclusive institute. While studying, Sarah used mediums like charcoals and watercolors, but in prison, she was forced to put her creativity to work.

Instead of typical art supplies, Sarah incorporates everyday materials like mascara or lipstick to color her pieces. A sketch of her sister was completed on a meticulously unfolded plain white envelope. And even without an artist's usual tools, Sarah's artistic talent even earned her praise from prosecutor Thomas Testa, who had argued that the "murderer" deserved to remain in prison for her full sentence.

Testa had even voiced concern that, with her innovative artistic ability, Sarah Dutra would be the next in a long history of criminals who cashed in on their infamy to build a name – and earn money – through art. In the past, online auctions have pulled in significant amounts for pieces created by murderers – cult leader Charles Manson's paintings, artwork by child murderer John Wayne Gacy Jr., or a greeting card hand-drawn by California mass murderer Dorothea Puente.

In an attempt to sway the court into releasing Sarah Dutra from prison, her defense attorney presented two of her pieces at the hearing

– attempting to showcase the more human side of a woman whose "unparalleled callousness" had been emphasized in the past. One of these works was a large oil painting of a scene at a café, while the other piece – the sketch on the unfolded enveloped – was of Sarah's younger sister Rachel in Yosemite Valley, holding her arms out to her sides while riding a bicycle.

With Sarah ordered to pay a large amount of money to her victims, Testa said he worried the young artist might try to secretly earn a profit off her artwork while serving time in prison.

"I hope I'm wrong," he said, admitting he appreciated the piece Sarah had done of her sister in Yosemite. "If her art does fetch a price, that should go where the judge ordered it."

But according to Sarah's attorney, San Joaquin County Deputy Public Defender Keith Arthur, there are currently no artworks of hers in circulation – as far as he knew, anyway. He said while he has no education or knowledge of art, he could see some of Sarah's personal struggles depicted through the contrast of the lighting in her café scene.

"The value they had to me is that prison did not crush her spirit," he said. "She's still struggling toward the light, like we all do."

This idea is part of why many prisoners tend to turn inward and explore their artistic sides while living behind bars, according to Ed Mead, a former prisoner in Washington who now runs a website where inmates can sell their works. Mead said art "gives prisoners a skill and sense of self-worth."

"You keep them in a cage day in and day out and expect them to come out better people," he said.

JoDee Bebout, who was married to Larry McNabney and mothered his two grown children, has remarried and forgiven Sarah Dutra for her role in Larry's death – but doesn't understand why anyone would ever want to own a piece of artwork created by a convicted killer. If Sarah hadn't killed her ex-husband, JoDee said, no one would know her name – and her pieces, no matter how good, would have no value.

"It gave me an icky chill," she said of Sarah's café scene painting presented in court. "Now that she's a high-profile killer, maybe there's a weirdo out there who may buy it."

A made-for-TV movie called "Lies My Mother Told Me" was based on the case. The film, which aired in 2005 on Lifetime, featured Joely Richardson as Elisa, Kailin See as Sarah, and Hayden Panettiere as Elisa's daughter Haylei.

"We, as his children, are working on forgiveness for our health and well-being," Williams said, following the announcement that Sarah Dutra would be released on parole.

THE VALENTINES DAY MURDER

ANA BENSON

Richard and Stacy Schoeck had a perfect marriage, or at least it looked ideal for their friends and family. Even though they have been together for a long time, they seemed to have eyes only for each other. Richard was Stacy's fifth husband and everyone was certain that he was indeed the love of her life. The couple still went on dates and celebrated their love in every way possible. So when Valentine's Day in 2010 came around, the Schoecks were setting up a romantic little getaway and a card exchange in a picturesque Belton Bridge Park which is located in Lula, Georgia.

Lula is a quiet little tourist town so when their Police Department received a frantic phone call with Stacy on the other end of the line, they knew something serious had happened. The town was shocked to discover that a murder occurred right there in their calm little oasis. But soon enough, the sinister plot started to unravel and the law enforcement realized that things were not as they seemed.

So what made Stacy Schoeck turn on her loving husband and who helped her with the murderous plan?

Early life

Stacy Morgan was born in 1971 in Florida. Her childhood wasn't perfect at all and her father died when she was really young. This left a permanent mark on Stacy even though her mother remarried soon and she did have a father figure in her life. She was also molested during this time frame by an individual who remained anonymous to everyone around her. Stacy grew up to be a lovely teenage girl who would fall in love easily. She met her first husband while she was still in high school and the couple got married shortly after. Unfortunately, he wasn't what Stacy was looking for and it took her two years to come to this conclusion. She filed for a divorce and the two separated.

When Stacy was twenty years old, she met her second husband. Soon after the wedding, Stacy found out that she was pregnant with her first child. The marriage lasted a little more than a year and she once again filed for a divorce when her son was just a toddler. Instead of being beaten down by two failed marriages, Stacy remained strong and made a decision to improve herself. After all, she was only twenty-two years old. She applied for college and got accepted. Stacy moved on to raise her son on her own and earn a degree in psychology and nursing at the same time.

She managed to find the employment as soon as she got out of college. Stacy was still very optimistic about her love life and wanted to find someone to spend the rest of her life with. She met her third husband in 1997 but unfortunately, the marriage was short-lived once again. It lasted for only six weeks. Stacy decided to date casually in the future and gave birth to her second son in 1998. She was still a single mother but this didn't seem to bother her at all.

Stacy did need to improve her financial status and she found a better job opportunity at a clinic which was located in Atlanta. The family moved over there and she was ready to start over. She got an excellent position at the hospital's administration with the possibility of even better promotion. She would assist the doctors on a daily basis with various tasks. Stacy was a successful and independent woman who was capable of taking care of her two small boys on her own.

But something was still missing and Stacy was longing for a partner who would be there for her. She was tired of casual encounters and needed some stability. So in 2001 she married for the fourth time and moved out to a small town near Atlanta. She got pregnant once again and gave birth to her third son. She lived in a large house with her fourth husband and it seemed that her life was absolutely perfect. Her boys were happy and they loved the suburban lifestyle. On the other hand, Stacy was still unhappy. Soon after the separation from her fourth husband in 2005, Stacy met Richard Schoeck, a graphic designer who was slightly older than her. He was a patient at the hospital where Stacy worked at the time. The two hit it off immediately.

Richard Schoeck was an adventurer who lived his life to the maximum. Stacy was immediately attracted to his positive attitude and passionate outlook. Richard accepted Stacy's sons like they were his own and would often organize family outings that included the entire family. She loved how different Richard was from all of her previous husbands and thought that she had finally found the one.

Unconcerned about Stacy's previous failed marriages, Richard still wanted to make their relationship permanent. The couple did get married in 2007 but the ceremony wasn't standard at all. Stacy and Richard eloped and told everyone about the wedding once they came back home. It was in Richard's nature to do something so spontaneous and Stacy adored him for that.

Richard became a stay at home dad after the wedding and he would form a close bond with Stacy's boys. He was very involved with their school and hobbies so he ended up adopting the youngest two. He really did accept this small family as his own and wanted the best for the boys. Everyone approved of Richard and Stacy's family hoped that she finally found the man of her life. Unfortunately, this marriage would end up tragically in just a couple of years.

The murder of Richard Schoeck

Prior to Valentine's Day in February of 2010, Stacy invited Richard on a small romantic getaway to the town of Lulu, Georgia. They were supposed to meet in Belton Bridge Park which is a secluded area near the town itself and exchange gifts there. This wasn't unusual for the Schoecks because they would often go on different adventures that were supposed to spice up their love life. The Police dispatchers received a frantic phone call sometime after the nightfall. Stacy was screaming that her husband was shot and robbed. He wasn't showing any signs of life.

The police arrived at the scene of the crime and sure enough, Richard's body was lying next to his pickup truck. The blood was both inside and outside of the vehicle which meant that several shots were fired. At least one bullet hit him while he was still in the driver's seat or getting out of the car. He crawled out, perhaps to run away or defend himself. The shooter continued firing the gun until they were certain that Richard was dead.

The investigators immediately closed off the area and examined the tire tracks which were visible in the surrounding mud. They noticed that the third vehicle was definitely there and that it left the scene of the crime prior to the arrival of Stacy. The law enforcement marked them as the evidence. However, there were some red flags that indicated that this wasn't a standard robbery. For instance, Richard's valet was still in the car and his jewelry was on him. Nothing was taken from the scene.

Stacy wasn't a suspect at the time but the police escorted her to the station in order to interview her and get as many details as possible. Lulu is a quiet town where crime rarely happens so the law enforcement couldn't zero in on any possible reason why Richard was shot. One theory suggested that he might have interrupted another couple at Belton Bridge Park because it was a common meeting ground for lovebirds who wanted to spend some time together outside of their homes.

The interviews and investigation

Once Stacy got to the station, she started talking. She was asked to explain what they were doing at the remote park and she admitted that they did have problems in their marriage. She thought this would be the perfect time to add some flare to their relationship. Since Richard was a stay at home dad and she had difficult work hours, the two simply couldn't get any alone time to spend with each other. She was becoming desperate and unhappy.

She quickly admitted to having an affair to the shock of everyone who was present in the interrogation room. Her lover was a fellow co-worker from the hospital who was significantly younger than Richard. His name was Juan and he was a complete opposite of Stacy's husband. She needed intimacy and she fell in love with someone else who could give her everything she craved for. Stacy even took her lover to Las Vegas just a couple of weeks prior to the murder of her husband.

The detectives were interested in the affair and started asking questions related to the possibility that Stacy wanted to get out of her marriage with Richard in order to be with her new man. Stacy told them that she did think about leaving Richard but that no particular plans were made. She knew how much her children loved him and getting a divorce would probably break their hearts. They focused on Stacy's lover but she quickly debunked their claims by saying that he is not violent at all and that she cannot imagine him being involved with anything involving guns or shooting.

But Stacy did say that Juan knew about the rendezvous in the park so the police decided to call him up for an interview the next morning. Juan seemed oblivious to the events that took place last night and he told the detectives that Stacy claimed her relationship with Richard was open. This meant that each of them had someone on the side. Juan didn't seem to be bothered by this arrangement at all so the investigators started doubting their possible theory. Plus, Juan had a solid alibi for the time of the murder because he was in another city.

They were left without any solid lead in this case so it was time to look a bit further and include as much aid as possible. The park is a fairly isolated place but there was a nearby cell phone tower that covered the entire area. The investigators knew that if a call was placed from that location on the night of the murder, they would have the number listed. And it turned out that this was a crucial move made by the investigators because it would lead them in the right direction.

The list of calls was short because that cell tower is not in an urban area. The detectives used the contact information which was stored in both Stacy's and Richard's phones and they tried to find the match. Stacy's phone had the number that was called sometime around the murder. The contact info itself stood out because it said Mr. Results. The investigators were slightly confused because they had no idea who this person was. But calling him up would probably shed some light on the events that occurred on Valentine's Day.

The police quickly identified the mystery man who was present at the scene of the crime that night. His name was Reginald Coleman and he worked as a private fitness instructor in Atlanta. Coleman was born in Philadelphia but his criminal past led him to move out from his hometown and try to start over in another state. He was incarcerated in the past but managed to clean up his act. Coleman was doing fine financially and owned a fairly popular gym. As far as the local police force knew, he was staying away from any type of crime.

Todd Woodten who would become Coleman's attorney during the trial said the following on his client: "Reginald was a true survivor. He was street-savvy and always had a hustle going on. He did a lot of things for youth, trying to keep them off the street and keep them safe."

Once the police managed to attain the call records from Reginald Coleman's cell phone, they found the number he had called from the Belton Bridge Park. The investigators thought they would see Stacy Schoeck's digits but they were surprised with their discovery. Coleman called another woman - Lynitra Ross. The detectives then realized that the whole plot was more complicated that they initially assumed and that there are more players involved with the murder of Richard Schoeck. So how did all of them fit together?

After speaking to Coleman's friends, the police found out that Lynitra Ross was his ex-girlfriend who would often resurface in his life. But there was another detail that connected Lynitra to the murder – she worked at the same hospital as Stacy Schoeck and two of them were really good friends. Stacy was Lynitra's boss and a landlord. Since there was a third set of tire marks on the scene of the murder, the detectives quickly determined that the model did not fit the tires on Reginald's car. This did sidetrack them a bit but they were still determined to find out what really happened.

The investigators were certain that they did, in fact, have their suspect and that was Stacy Schoeck. However, they still had to connect the dots so they dug even further into the phone records of those three. There was a message exchange on the night prior to the murder of Richard Schoeck between the three parties. However, the most interesting clue was Stacy's bank account which clearly stated that she sent a total of $10,000 to Lynitra's account which she passed along to Reginald.

The arrests

Since the topic of the third vehicle was still the big unknown, the police started going through all cars which were somehow related to Stacy, Lynitra, and Reginald. And soon enough they were onto something. Stacy did have one car which she sold soon after the murder. It wasn't registered to her but she did use it often in order to drive her relatives or get them groceries. They were surprised to find out that Stacy put their vehicle on the market but she told them that they will get a newer model as a gift from her.

The police became very suspicious of this story so they tracked down the new owner and took a look at the tires as well as the insides of the car. And yes, the tire marks matched perfectly. Stacy Schoeck borrowed that car to Reginald Coleman on that fatal Valentine's Day. The evidence against Coleman was piling up and he was arrested on May 25th, 2010. But as soon as the interrogation started, he denied any involvement with Stacy Schoeck or the murder of her husband.

Lynitra Ross was arrested a couple of hours after Reginald but she also refused to provide the investigators with any useful information. It was time to pick up Stacy as well so the police arrived at the medical center she worked at and led her straight to the station. The investigators had plenty of circumstantial evidence to accuse her of the murder and they didn't have to wait for her accomplices to start talking about the crime. All three of them were in custody and it was time to face the justice for their actions.

Psychological assessment

Stacy Schoeck was put through a psychological assessment prior to the trial itself in order to determine if she had any underlying problems which were unknown to her or her family. The murder was well planned so she clearly wasn't distraught at the time which meant that Stacy knew exactly what she was doing when she asked her friend Lynitra to help her get rid of her husband.

The psychologists took a closer look at her prior relationships and marriages which ended in divorce. The reason for her unhappiness might lay in the fact that she lost her biological father when she was young and she was unable to connect to anyone. Not to forget that Stacy was also molested when she was just a child.

It was obvious that Stacy Schoeck was manipulative and knew how to get exactly what she wanted in every situation. Her intelligence was obviously high because she did put herself through school and successfully earned her degrees. However, her actions towards Richard Schoeck show that Stacy was also a sociopath because she hired a man to murder her husband and continued to live her life as nothing happened.

She mourned her husband publicly and got very emotional in front of her friends and family every time they saw her. The fact that she selected Valentine's Day as the date of the execution speaks volumes about her cold-heartedness towards Richard Schoeck.

The trials of Ross and Coleman

The first of three to stand a trial was Lynitra Ross. She entered the courtroom in May 2012 and was facing charges for a murder. After all, she was a co-conspirator who helped Stacy Schoeck find the hitman who would eventually pull the trigger and take Richard's life. Stacy was also present in the courtroom but she wasn't the accused in this situation. As a matter of fact, she testified on the side of the prosecution.

Stacy Schoeck was cooperating with the law enforcement and made a deal regarding her sentencing. She did everything to avoid the death penalty and was ready to talk about the murder of her husband. It was clear that her deeds were out in the open and she said the following as she took the stand: "I'm going to testify truthfully for Richard. It's all I can give his mom and his family and the children — all I can give them is the truth."

The jury then heard the story about the murder plot. Stacy Schoeck had the idea to take her husband's life in December 2009 after she noticed that her boys were acting strangely. They were getting into troubles and she started to suspect that they might be victims of molestation. She remembered how she behaved during the time she was assaulted as a child and found the connection. Of course, her first suspect was Richard because he was always with the boys.

Stacy also said: "I was just so fixated in my mind that Richard was doing something wrong that I said, 'I don't want the cops, I don't want a divorce, I want him dead.'" She then admitted to asking an unnamed man to help her kill her husband but he stopped returning her calls. Then she talked to her friend and co-worker Lynitra Ross and told her about her suspicions. Lynitra responded with the suggestion that they talk to her ex-boyfriend who would know what to do because he was "an experienced hitman".

After Lynitra Ross contacted Coleman, the two woman drove to his house and sat down with him in order to agree on some finer details regarding the hit. They talked and ate food from Zaxby's. Stacy suggested the park as the perfect place for executing her husband because he wouldn't suspect a thing. Reginald and Stacy agreed on the amount of money she would pay him for the murder, as well as on the vehicle he would take to the park. All three of them went to Belton Bridge Park so that Stacy could show him the exact place where her husband will be waiting.

Stacy noted in her testimony the following: "The only times I ever saw or spoke to Reginald Coleman was the day we had Zaxby's that afternoon and the following Saturday when we went up to Belton

Bridge. Everything else was done through Lynitra." She also added that she had given Lynitra the property she was renting to her as the payment for the help.

Lynitra's defense lawyers took the stand and told the jury that Stacy's testimony which involved the molestation claims was slightly off due to the fact that she admitted to having an affair in the first interview she gave after the murder. She didn't mention anything related to the possible sexual abuse of her children.

In August of 2012, Lynitra Ross was sentenced to life in prison. There would be no possibility of a parole either. Even though she didn't pull the trigger, she was the person who set up Stacy and Reginald to meet. Therefore, she was directly involved in the murder plot.

It was later determined that Richard Schoeck didn't have anything to do with child molestation but Stacy's plan was already completed and her husband was dead. The investigators took her claims seriously and talked to the middle boy who immediately said that he never accused Richard of anything. As a matter of fact, he never even talked to his mother about the alleged abuse. However, this didn't stop Stacy's attorneys from building their case around this.

Reginald Coleman's trial didn't last long because as soon as he appeared in front of the judge in November of 2012, he pleaded guilty to the murder of Richard Schoeck. He also faced charges for owning the firearm as a convicted felon. Stacy Schoeck was set to testify against him as well, which meant providing the courtroom with the full account of Reginald's actions.

Reginald Coleman agreed to kill Richard Schoeck after he heard the story of the alleged molestation directly from Stacy and Lynitra. Since he grew up in foster care, he often listened to the stories from his friends about their own abuse. Coleman thought that he could help the boys have a normal childhood by eliminating the threat from their life. He pleaded guilty in order to avoid the death penalty which was already on the table if he went on a trial. Coleman received the punishment of life in prison without the possibility of a parole and some additional years for the possession of the firearm.

Stacy Schoeck's trial

Once Ross and Coleman received their sentences, it was time for Stacy to appear in court for her own trial. The proceedings began in December of 2012 at Hall County Courtroom. Since Stacy cooperated with the prosecution in the trials of Coleman and Ross, the death penalty was off the table. Judge Jason Deal listened to the witnesses who described Richard Schoeck as a loving father and an exceptional friend who would never harm anyone. Stacy's defense attorneys once again repeated the story of the alleged abuse and claimed that her actions were severe because she wanted to protect her children from the aggressor.

When Stacy took the stand, she admitted to the crime and asked the judge to give her mercy. The defense told the courtroom about Stacy's own abuse and that she was acting erratically. However, the fact that the murder was planned months before it happened painted a picture of someone who wanted to eliminate her husband. Stacy had plenty of time to make sure that Richard was really the abuser and contact the law enforcement but she failed to do so.

Stacy's lawyers asked Judge Deal to consider giving Stacy a possibility of a parole and to keep in mind her troubled past. They also pointed out that Stacy was behaving well in prison and that she deserves a second chance. However, she received the punishment of life in prison without a chance to get out after serving thirty years which was the primary goal of her defense team.

Attorney Lee Darragh who led the prosecution said: "Judge Jason Deal appropriately recognized that Stacey Schoeck was the engine that put this train in motion, until the death of her husband. Without her involvement, this would not have occurred." The courtroom was filled with emotions because a large number of Richard's friends showed up for the hearing. One of the saddest moments was when Stacy's mother read a note which was written by her youngest boy which said: "I miss her every hour of every day, just like Daddy Richard."

Initially, Stacy Schoeck and Lynitra Ross were placed in two separate prisons in order to avoid any possible conflicts between the two but they were soon moved to the same facility – Pulaski State Prison. Stacy's family was left to wonder what was really the reason for this heinous crime because the exact motive was never uncovered. They got the custody of Stacy's three sons.

COLD BLOODED KILLER
CHRISTINA WALTERS

29

JENNIFER MARTIN

Christina "Shea" Walters: Cold Blooded Killer or Victim of Circumstance?

The Crime

It was a typical, hot August North Carolina night on August 17, 1998. Eighteen-year-old Tracy Lambert and her twenty-one-year-old friend, Susan Moore, were planning a night out on the town. The two vibrant, young blondes did their hair and make-up together and made plans to meet with friends. They got into Moore's car, and headed out toward their meeting place.

Suddenly, they were being tailed by an angry group of young strangers. The strangers were waving guns out the window, flashing their headlights, and yelling. Moore attempted to flee the group, but in a moment of terrified disorientation, she pulled down a dead-end road. Three young men approached the vehicle with guns drawn and forced the women into the trunk of Moore's car. The vehicle began moving with one of the young men behind the steering wheel. When it stopped, the men opened the trunk and demanded the women hand over their jewelry. Once all the jewelry was taken from the women, the trunk was again closed and the car began moving once again.

The second time the car stopped, the trunk was opened to reveal a larger group against the back drop of a trailer park. The group began discussing how to "dispose" of the women, causing Lambert to cry out and plead for mercy. A young American Indian woman expressed disgust with Lambert's "pathetic whimpering," and slammed the trunk door back shut. The men piled back into Moore's car while the rest of the group got into a second vehicle. The cars followed one another into an open, rural area where Lambert and Moore were forced out of the car. Each of the women was dragged into the open by one of the men who had committed the carjacking. Moore began pleading for their lives. She reportedly asked the men, "What are you going to do to us? Are you going to kill us?" She followed the question by trying to compromise, stating, "We don't know what you look like. Just let us go." At that point, one man held a gun to Tracy Lambert's head and said, "Well, I'm about to open this bitch's third eye." Lambert then started crying and said, "Oh, my god, Susan. We're going to die. We're going to die. I don't want to die." The gunman then told Tracy to "Shut up" before shooting her in the head. Another man was holding onto Moore with a knife to her throat as she watched her friend be killed. She began sobbing and begged him not to cut her throat, offering to him that he could just shoot her, instead. He showed mercy in that one small instance and borrowed the gun from his friend, ending her life instantly.

By midnight, friends and family were already concerned that the women had not arrived at the social gathering and began to look. An anonymous phone call alerted the police that the caller had "seen some people get shot." Sometime around dawn, the bodies were reported as discovered.

Earlier that same night, Debra Cheeseborough was leaving work at Bojangles when a young man, his face hidden beneath a bandana, approached her, placed a gun to her side, and told her if she'd cooperate, he would not hurt her. He ordered her into the trunk of her own car, where she lay still, quietly praying as a group of young people, all unidentifiable beneath their bandana masks, climbed into her car and began driving. Presumably as they dug through the contents of her purse and glove box, one of the young men came to the realization that he had gone to school with Debra's daughter.

Debra felt a glimmer of hope in that instant. She thought that, maybe, because they had made a connection, they would let her go without harming her. That hope was crushed when she heard the young people joking about how they had disliked her daughter and how much fun it was going to be to get rid of her mother.

The group pulled the car into an isolated area of Fort Bragg and ordered Debra from the trunk. She cried and pleaded for her life to no avail. Several of the young people, each with their own gun, began firing bullets into her. She was shot all over her body until the group was confident that she was dead. They left her lying on the ground and drove away in her car.

Debra later testified that, as she laid in the field, she could hear the voice of her deceased mother comforting her. "She told me it wasn't my time yet," she said under oath. "She told me she was going to help me get to the road, but not too close where someone could hit me." Debra did manage to drag herself to the roadside, where she was spotted by a passing motorist. She survived her injuries that night and went on to testify against her attackers in court, ultimately putting many of them away for life.

The night of August 17, 1998 was, no doubt, life altering for all parties involved in the events that unfolded in Fayetteville, North Carolina. This included twenty-year-old Christina "Shea" Walter. On the night of the crime spree, Christina had gathered at her trailer home at 1386 Davis Street in Fayetteville along with friends Francisco Tirado, Eric Queen, John Juarbe, Tameika Douglas, Ione Black, Carlos Nevills, Darryl Tucker, and Carlos Frink. Having grown up on the "wrong side of the tracks," all nine of the young people who gathered at the trailer had aligned themselves with the "Crip" gang, although they each claimed different "sets" or subgroups of the gang. The subgroups had come together and realized that the gang, as a whole, was in need of money. They formulated a plan to steal a car and drive it through the front window of a pawn shop, where they would steal the inventory.

Earlier in the afternoon, the nine friends had gone to Wal-Mart. They bought bullets with which they were going to carry out their plan and stole clothing and toiletries. When they arrived back at the trailer,

Tirado borrowed Christina's blue fingernail polish to color the tips of the bullets blue. This was symbolic, the group agreed, of the "Crips" gang.

After discussing their plan, the group split up. Christina, Douglas, Nevills, and Black called a friend to drive them into a quiet neighborhood. Christina gave Nevills a gun and told him to find a victim and put them in the trunk of a car, then return to her trailer within an hour and a half.

Debra Cheeseborough was their first victim.

After the group thought they had killed Cheeseborough, they returned to Christina's trailer where they discussed their plan further. They realized that they needed another car. Christina, Tucker, Black, and Queen took Cheeseborough's car in search of another victim, ultimately finding Tracy Lambert and Susan Moore.

After killing the two young women, the group decided to call it a night and meet up at the trailer the next day. However, Tirado had trouble sleeping and kept one ear to the police scanner all night. At around dawn, he called Christina and reported to her that bodies had been found. From there, the entire group, with the exception of Black and Nevills, fled to Myrtle beach in Cheeseborough and Moore's cars, using her cell phone to place calls back to family and friends.

On Tuesday, August 18th, police in Myrtle Beach arrested Juarbe and Tucker and impounded Cheeseborough's car. The next day, they received an anonymous tip that Christina had rented a room at the Bona Villa motel in Myrtle Beach. They checked out the tip and found Moore's car in the parking lot. There, they apprehended Christina, Frink, Douglas, Queen, and Tirado. Soon, there was a media frenzy.

The Outcry

Throughout Fayetteville, the deaths of Lambert & Moore and the brutally savage attack on Debra Cheeseborough left the community enraged. The news that the crime spree was related to gang activity created a frenzy of individuals calling to "clean up the streets." News outlets flashed pictures of Moore and Lambert, two white, blonde haired, beautiful young ladies, but were less inclined to show images of Debra Cheeseborough, a middle-aged black woman. This, according to the defense, fed into a racial divide. Without knowing that Cheeseborough was a minority woman, herself, many within Fayetteville believed the violence was a hate crime against white people, instigated by a violent gang of minority youths. The fact that the attacks had been random was lost in the coverage and, soon, Fayetteville found itself in the throes of racial and economic divide.

The Woman

Not much is known about Christina's life before the events that unfolded that fateful night in 1998. Based on statements presented to her attorney, we can surmise that Christina's upbringing was less than ideal. She has made claims of being abused physically, emotionally, and sexually as a child. In one story, which would later come back to haunt her during trial, she spoke of cutting a man with a box cutter as he was trying to sexually abuse her.

As is the case with a lot of youths who feel displaced from their families and communities, Christina sought the embrace of whatever makeshift form of family she could find. In her case, she fell into a crowd of similarly dysfunctional minority youths who claimed membership to one of the largest street gangs in America: The Crips.

As Christina reached adulthood, she was able to secure her own place to live, which opened up a meeting ground for herself and fellow gang members to congregate in. Because her home was often the meeting point, she found herself in the position of leader and would often have to assert her dominance over other gang members who tried to challenge her. There is little doubt that the control Christina found within the gang was a welcome change from her helpless childhood. Christina no doubt realized that, in her newly given position, she could find safety in her power. She became a fearless leader of her group and was unafraid to assert herself with dominance or even threats of death.

Until that August night, though, Christina had never actually killed anyone. As would be explained in court by her co-defendants, to kill someone for the good of the gang is one of the highest honors the Crips had established at the time. The honor was memorialized with a teardrop tattoo on the face following a "confirmed kill."

Christina saw the carjacking plan as an opportunity to earn the highest honor she could for her gang, securing herself a position of leadership for life. To those of us who have grown up in more mild environments, it seems to be an act of selfishness and a fool's errand. To Christina, though, it would mean a lifetime of security from anyone that would ever attempt to cause her pain.

As the gang made plans to secure funds for their needs, Christina made plans of her own.

As the events unfolded, Christina remained mostly quiet about her intent to kill the carjacking victims. As each of the cars were stolen, the women were brought back to Christina's trailer to discuss their fates. It was only then that Christina expressed her desire for the women to be killed.

To refuse to kill someone for the benefit of the gang would have been suicide. With no other option but to help Christina, the co-defendants carried out Christina's plan alongside her. Because they had done so, Christina was responsible for helping them attempt to escape punishment, which is why she paid the way for everyone to go to Myrtle Beach.

Some of Christina's supporters today make a case that Christina wasn't cold-blooded. She was simply living the only life she knew how to survive in, and that her case was unnecessarily worsened by the media attention and dishonesty of news outlets at the time. Rumors regarding Christina's character and the lifestyle of the gang itself began to circulate. Soon enough, the story had evolved into a tale that Christina forced the co-defendants to kill two white women as a form of initiation into the gang. This was simply not the truth, but it was a tale that the defense had trouble running from. In the end, Christina "Shea" Walters believed the rumors and unfair media exposure were responsible for the severity of her sentencing.

The Trial

Regardless of Christina's culpability, she suffered from having inadequate representation at her trial. She was advised that, because of the media attention surrounding the case, the courts would issue a change of venue and try her somewhere other than Fayetteville. Unbeknownst to her, she would have had to file a motion for the change of venue. By the time she realized the need for her to initiate the motion, it was too late to file and her case was stuck at the center of a media whirlwind.

Because of the public nature of the case, Christina believes she was unable to receive a fair trial. According to her defense, eight of the twelve jurors that were seated on the jury had already been informed of the details of her case by other potential jurors and courtroom staff prior to the trial beginning. The state of North Carolina rebutted this claim stating that each juror swore to be fair and impartial and to disregard any information they had heard or read prior to the beginning of the proceedings. The state also argues that Christina never objected to the jurors at the appropriate time when she should have. Christina argues that, again, her defense team failed her and she did not know her rights.

She also claims she did not know her rights when she failed to file a motion for the murders of Lambert and Moore to be tried separately from the attack on Cheeseborough. Trying the crimes at the same time, she says, is partly to blame for the outcome of the proceedings.

Probably one of Christina's most compelling arguments that she did not receive a fair trial, however, comes with evidence logged right into the court report, itself. During the selection of the jurors, the Judge actually left the court room. During that time, a reporter began interviewing a potential juror about the case. The transcript reads as follows;

Judge: And, Madam Clerk, would you go ahead and call another juror please for number five?

Clerk: Richard Council.

Judge: Thank you. Counsel, I have to make a phone call to my district attorney. If you'll give me just a moment, please? (Leaves courtroom)

(Number five, Mr. Council, enters court room.)

Bailiff: Sir, come on up and have a seat in number five.

(A male media representative was talking to the juror, Mr. Council, as the juror walked by.)

Court Reporter: Tell that guy to quit talking to the juror- that media guy.

(Bailiff, Sgt. David Farrell, directed number five, Mr. Council, in the box after Sgt. Farrell spoke to the media representative.)

(Judge returns to courtroom.)

Judge: Remain seated.

Bailiff: Come to order. Court's in session.

Christina argues that, because the media had time to address the juror, and because nobody in the court room bothered to inform the Judge of the interaction, the juror was tampered with prior to the beginning of the proceedings and had already been given an "insider's idea" of what the hope of the community was for the outcome of her case.

Finally, Christina says that her past was brought up in court unnecessarily, with facts "twisted" to make her seem like a more brutal and violent person than she really believes herself to be. This is where the case falls back to the instance of self- defense against a sexual predator. Again, the evidence is in the transcript:

Prosecutor: Did you say your dad almost killed a boy that you stabbed?

Christina: I haven't stabbed no boy.

Prosecutor: Did you say that?

Christina: No, ma'am. I don't remember saying anything like that.

Prosecutor: Do you remember saying the boy you stabbed was 20-something at the time?

Christina: Unless the person who wrote this was talking about when I had a boyfriend who was trying to take my shirt off and I sliced him with a box cutter, but that's not stabbing.

At this point in the trial, the Judge did excuse the jury momentarily to ask the prosecutor why they were asking these questions. During the conversation, the Judge asked the defense why he had not objected to the questioning, clearly recognizing that it was a bad direction for the defense to allow the questioning to go.

Failing Christina, yet again, the defense attorney responded, "Well, because we didn't care at the point she was at."

One has to wonder- if a judge sees a line of questioning that is so outrageous he will dismiss the jury and ask, himself, why nobody is objecting to it- how does the defense, itself, not recognize the issue? Christina's supporters say that she was being defended by a court-appointed attorney who, they claim, was already swayed by the media outcry against Christina. He did not wish for her to win her case, so he did not even try to offer her a solid defense.

During the same testimony, Christina admitted that she shot several .32 caliber bullets into Cheeseborough, only stopping once she thought the victim was dead. Cheeseborough was able to testify against Walters, although she stated in her testimony that she could not positively identify her shooters. In appeals, Christina has stated that she was not well- advised by her attorney and only confessed to attempting to kill Cheeseborough because she believed that, because the victim of her shooting had survived, she would not be tied to the deaths of the other two women.

His failure to object to the unfair questioning, compiled with his failure to alert the judge of the jury tampering and not clearly outlining

Christina's rights to her prior to trial are all signs indicating that, perhaps, Christina and her followers may be correct in their assumption.

In July of 2000, the trial came to a close with Christina Walters sentenced to Death. Eric Queen and Paco Tirado were both also sentenced to death in the months prior. With the ruling, Christina became the fifth woman on North Carolina's death row and secured herself a place as one of the state's most notorious female killers.

While there is little doubt that the acts committed against Tracy Lambert, Susan Moore, and Debra Cheeseborough on that August night were horrendous and cruel, there is reason to question whether or not Walters received a fair trial and sentencing in accordance with her legal rights under Federal law. Around the country, as news of the court case spread, Walters acquired supporters who felt empathy for her unfortunate upbringing and believed that she had been "railroaded" in court. As her following grew, the case began receiving attention from a new light, ultimately leading to a re-examination of the facts.

The Commuted Sentence

In December of 2012, a North Carolina judge commuted Christina Walters's death sentence along with the death sentences of two other convicted killers as part of the scaling back of the Racial Justice Act. The decision in each of the three cases came after a four-week deliberation on their individual cases in which the prosecution was proven to have made a conscious and indisputable error to reduce the number of black jurors in the original trials.

Although each of the prosecutors argued that they had, in fact, not made any such effort, the judge said that it was ultimately their own mannerisms and testimony that proved otherwise. "The conclusion is based primarily on the words and deeds of prosecutors involved in these cases," he said. "Despite presentations to the contrary, their words, their deeds, speak volumes. During presentation of evidence, the court finds powerful and persuasive evidence of racial consciousness, race-based decision making in the writings of prosecutors long buried in the case files and brought to light for the first time during this hearing."

Christina Walters, a Lumbee Indian, having been proven to have been tried unfairly based on her race, was commuted from death row to a life sentence without the possibility of parole.

The Repeal

In December of 2015, the Supreme Court vacated the commute claiming that the Judge did not give prosecutors adequate time to respond to a statistical study on race in the North Carolina state court system. The Racial Justice Act was also overturned, causing Christina Walters to, once again, have to appeal her case.

The study referenced concluded in 2011 showed that racial bias played a role in culling jurors before death penalty trials. Prosecutors disagreed with the claims, stating that the race of the juror doesn't play a role in their decision for keeping or releasing someone from the jury selection panel. The study examined 173 capital trials over a 20-year period to accumulate evidence to the contrary.

Qualified black jurors were over twice as likely to be released from panels under peremptory strikes according to Michigan State University's study of capital cases ranging from 1990 to 2010. Prosecutors argued that the study was invalid because the range of statistics stretched out far too broadly, failing to present an accurate depiction of how jurors are currently selected.

The Supreme Court encouraged both sides to prevent additional studies to support their claims.

In January of 2017, Christina Walters's legal team appealed her death sentence by using the now-repealed Racial Justice Act. Prosecutors argued that she couldn't use the repealed act because it has been repealed. Her defense argued that she had obtained relief under the Act and that it was unfair to strip her of that relief retroactively.

Judge Spainhour from Raleigh, North Carola presided over the case. He decided that Christina Walters's case was still pending under the Racial Justice Act and, therefore she could no longer use the repealed act.

There is little doubt that Christina Walters and her supporters will continue to appeal their case in pursuit of a commuted sentence or a retrial. With the buzz surrounding the case, it's hard not to look at the entirety of the situation objectively to determine if Christina is really the cold and calculated killer that prosecution in the original trial portrayed her to be or if, instead, she is a young woman led astray by circumstance, then railroaded by a court system designed to work against her.

Jay Ferguson, an attorney on her legal team, was quoted in the Fayetteville News Observer as saying, "We are confident that, no matter how many hearings are held or studies completed, we will win this case. The evidence of racial bias in jury selection is simply overwhelming and undeniable. All this decision will do is add more delays and cost the state millions to conduct new studies and hold new hearings. We will be throwing more taxpayer money into a hopelessly broken death penalty."

SERIAL KILLER DOCTOR : THE TRUE STORY OF ALICE WYNEKOOP

42

NATHAN NIXON

The Wynekoop Case

There are few murder cases in history that have been as bizarre as The Wynekoop case. Perhaps it is the circumstance of a mother allegedly committing an awful act for her son that grabbed so much attention. Maybe it was the sense among American's that such a seemingly sweet and noble woman could not possibly have committed such a crime. During a time in the United States that is already a tale of struggle and recovery, this murder set in 1933 stood in the headlines for weeks and gripped an entire class of people along the way. The story of Dr. Alice L. Wynekoop is one for the ages.

Alice Lindsay was born in 1870. Although little was recorded or known of her early life, it is well documented that she lived an absolutely normal childhood. The importance of The Wynekoop case begins with her marriage to Frank Wynekoop in the 1890's. Alice Lindsay took the famous name, now, of Alice Lindsay Wynekoop. She worked hard in her education in the medical field, and soon became a full practicing doctor in the late 1890's. By the turn of the century, Dr. Alice Wynekoop, along with her husband Frank Wynekoop, would start to put together the foundation for what would later become one of the Chicago area's most chilling scenes.

The beginning of this chilling case actually begins in 1901. Frank and Alice Wynekoop decided to supervise the construction of a massive red-bricked mansion in the west side of Chicago. Their thinking was to create a safe, family centered environment for their entire family. Soon after, the property was popularly said to be "cursed". Frank and Alice had several children. Their daughter, Marie Louise, died there inside the home in an upstairs bedroom. Frank's brother, Dr. Gilbert Wynekoop, put the entire family in the headlines when he attempted to strangle his unfaithful wife during their divorce proceedings. This was said to have happened in the family living room. Dr. Gilbert Wynekoop later was clinically diagnosed as insane and was institutionalized.

All of these dreadful event happened in a 20 year timespan leading up to the dreariest event of them all. Before the murder, the house was already tagged as haunted throughout the neighborhood. The Wynekoop's were ultimately the black sheep of the neighborhood. It is important to keep in mind the era that this is in. This was a time in American History when the totality of medical care was transitioning to major hospitals and medical establishments. There was still, however, significant medical care that was happening in local housing. The Wynekoop household fit this bill. They had several rooms in the house devoted to the family medical practice. There were rooms for operations and general care as well as a morgue in the basement. This was obviously well known in the neighborhood, and gave more material for the whispers around town to gossip about. Those whispers gained a much bigger voice in 1933.

Prior to 1933, there was actually some positivity toward Dr. Alice Wynekoop. While many spoke of the property being haunted and many in the neighborhood holding a genuine fear of going around the house, that opinion was not generally shared in regards to Frank and Alice Wynekoop. Dr. Alice Wynekoop was an influential figure in the women's suffrage movement as well as an advocate for women's rights as a whole. Alice graduated medical school from Northwestern University in Illinois. She was generally admired and held in high regard for her medical practicing in the area. She would commonly provide medical care to those in need when they may not have had the means to garner medical attention from other places. She was a one of the primary leaders in the evolution of child healthcare and believed wholeheartedly in fair, honest medical treatment of everyone, regardless of their income or ability to pay. For these reasons, the bizarre events of 1933 still have people split on what really happened. Dr. Alice Wynekoop, for all intents and purposes, could also be called a killer and a liar.

The relationship that Alice had with her son is of supreme importance to the case. Frank and Alice's son, Earle Wynekoop, was generally described as a low-life. Specifically, he desired to stay in the mansion as long as possible. He often leeched money off of Alice and Frank and was never really forced to grow up.

In 1929, Dr. Frank Wynekoop, the husband of Alice Wynekoop, passed away. This left the massive 16 bedroom mansion with only Alice Wynekoop, Earle Wynekoop, and Rheta Wynekoop, the wife of Earle.

Earle and Rheta Wynekoop had an unsuccessful marriage to say the least. After her death, a deep investigation was conducted by investigators into the past of Earle Wynekoop. Earle was said to have a "black book" with as many as 50 names in it. He frequented fairs, where he would set out to woo as many women as he could. He famously is said to have had "as many as 25 fiancée's" at one point in time. Many women who would later be questioned said that "he made love to them in the strangest and most repulsive ways." This would all lead to Rheta Wynekoop questioning their marriage. Rheta grew tremendously depressed and often times found herself in competition with Earle's lovers. She famously weighed herself as much as ten times per day.

Although Earle had fallen out of love with Rheta shortly after their honeymoon, the marriage continued in the oddest of circumstances. In 1933, the Wynekoop mansion housed Alice, Earle, Rheta, and a boarder or little significance to the case. The basement of the mansion was the site of great medical care as well as several other bedrooms in the house. This was an odd living situation for all involved.

Dr. Alice Wynekoop tried all that she could to support the marriage. Strangely enough, this repulsed Rheta even more. Rheta felt that Alice had "blind support" for Earle, regardless of what he did and how he did it. To supremely set the stage for baffling case, Alice had taken up life insurance policies on Rheta just weeks before her tragic death. Upon the death of Rheta Wynekoop, Alice was set to collect

$12,000, a staggering amount of money in the depression era in the early 1930's.

The overall situation of the Wynekoop's was a bit strange. With all of these things considered, it is no wonder how there could be reasonable suspicion raised about Dr. Wynekoop's part in a heinous crime. The events of the murder are both chilling and confusing. The night of November 21, 1933 will forever be an event that still has many questions surrounding it.

The Murder

It was around 10 P.M. that a police officer that was out on patrol was dispatched to the Wynekoop home. Who was the person who phoned police on that evening? Ironically enough, the caller was none other than Dr. Alice Wynekoop.

"Something terrible has happened," Dr. Alice Wynekoop said to police upon entering the home. "Come on downstairs and I will show you."

Officers would describe Alice Wynekoop as anxious and jittery. The officer notably referenced a calm in her voice, however.

The group made their way downstairs to the doctor's operating room in the Wynekoop home. Immediately upon entering the room, it was quickly clear that something wasn't quite right.

On a table in the center of the room lay a body. The body was still slightly warm to the touch and showed evidence of very recent death. A sheet had been thrown over the body, leaving only bare feet and the head and upper shoulders exposed. The face had numerous scratches on it, however nothing specifically deep or significant. There was moderate bruising over many parts of the body as well as discoloration on several areas of the flesh. It appeared as if there was some sort of struggle that took place before the body was placed on the table. This was the body of Rheta Wynekoop, wife of Earle Wynekoop and daughter in law off Dr. Alice Wynekoop.

Upon further examination of the body, it was quickly discovered that Rheta had suffered a gunshot wound through the back. With closer examination, the bullet was tracked to have entered the back just above the midline and to have taken an upward course through the torso. The bullet was lodged just beneath Rheta's left breast. After autopsy, the final exam would show that the entire thorax was filled with blood. The overall significance to investigators with this information was that it showed Rheta was alive when she was shot. This indicated that the official cause of death was the gunshot wound to her back causing hemorrhage and shock. The manner of death was officially ruled a homicide.

Autopsy also revealed a significant level of chloroform. Chloroform held many important medicinal uses, especially in the 1930's. A common anesthetic, chloroform was a popular choice among doctors as an agent to administer prior to a surgery. Investigation of the scene found a bottle of chloroform in the operatory room where Rheta was found. It was almost completely empty.

Also found at the crime scene was a revolver. The revolver showed signs that it had just been fired. There were also three displaced cartridges next to the revolver. This would prove to be the murder weapon. Oddly enough, the revolver belonged to Earle Wynekoop.

Earle Wynekoop would seem to have been a prime suspect upon the initial discovery of the body of Rheta. After all, he was in a marriage that he had no interest in being in. He had countless instances of unfaithfulness to support this theory. Rheta was unhappy with the marriage as well, as she knew of his acts outside of their marriage.

Earle Wynekoop was not at the house at the time of the murder according the Dr. Alice Wynekoop and others at the scene. Police questioned Earle and this statement was supported. Earle Wynekoop was driving to Arizona at the time of the murder. This led investigators to quickly eliminate him as a suspect in the murder. Dr. Wynekoop's daughter did not live in the house hold. She was a physician at Cook County Hospital. While Dr. Alice Wynekoop's daughter was present at the home at the time of the murder, it was professed to authorities by Alice Wynekoop that she was only asked for help after the body was discovered. Enid Hennessey, who was renting out a room at the house, was not accounted for at the time of the murder. She was quickly ruled out as a suspect as she had no connection to the family nor the murder beyond maintaining a temporary living arrangement.

This left only Dr. Alice Wynekoop as a suspect. Police initially marked her as the prime suspect being as she apparently identified the body first. According to Alice's initial information that she gave to police on scene, the other members of the household had no contact with Rheta and couldn't have possibly been involved.

Police quickly got a statement from Alice Wynekoop as to what happened that evening. This is truly where things get complicated in this case. Dr. Alice Wynekoop's first statement was, perhaps, a far-fetched effort to lead investigator's down a winding road that could not necessarily be disproven.

According to the first statement, Dr. Alice Wynekoop entered the operatory at precisely 8:30 P.M. to "obtain some medicine for flu-like symptoms for both her and Enid." As she arrived in the room, she saw Rheta lying on the table. Alice examined her and confirmed that she was dead. It was at this time that Dr. Alice Wynekoop called her daughter at the hospital and notified her of what happened. Catherine Wynekoop quickly came home from the hospital and pronounced Rheta dead.

It was at this time that a red flag was apparent to investigators. Rather than immediately notify police of what happened, Dr. Alice Wynekoop instead chose to call an undertaker.

Alice Wynekoop was questioned as to who could have committed this murder if all was true as she said. Dr. Wynekoop blamed the murder on thieves. She explained that there had been numerous instances that her home was broken into by thieves who were out to collect money and drugs from her operating rooms down stairs.

Police found this all to be quite misleading. If she indeed suspected that Rheta had been murdered by thieves in an apparent break in, why would she not call authorities upon discovering Rheta's body?

The deck was beginning to stack against Dr. Wynekoop. Police questioned her a second time a few days later. She gave a nearly identical statement that featured even more details of how she discovered the body. She attempted to explain to authorities that even if she had notified authorities, Rheta was already dead when she found her. This still, however, baffled police. Moreover, extensive crime scene investigation of all of the downstairs offices of the Wynekoop home showed that there was no evidence of a burglary and there was nothing that was missing to provide evidence of a burglary. This left everything pointing still toward Dr. Alice Wynekoop as the murderer of Rheta Wynekoop.

For all of these extensive reasons, police arrested Dr. Alice Wynekoop and charged her with the murder of her daughter-in-law, Rheta Wynekoop. It was at this time that Alice gave the chilling statement that would be used at trial. The statement she would give was a completely irrational argument that defied belief. This third official statement has long been seen as one of the most erratic and random stories to explain a crime in recent history.

Dr. Alice Wynekoop would go into detail about some of the habits of Rheta.

"Rheta was greatly concerned about her health and her overall appearance," Alice said in her statement. "She was always weighing herself, usually stripping down to the nude in order to do so. On Tuesday, November 21, after a luncheon, at about 1:00 P.M. she decided to go into town to buy some sheet music that she had long been wanting."

Police immediately knew that this was going to work its way into a confession. The statement was carefully taken. It was during the opening parts of her confession that police noticed that her story was already changing dramatically from anything she had stated before.

"Rheta had decided to weigh herself before she headed into town. I was working in the operatory. She was sitting on the table, practically naked. She complained that she had pain in her side that was causing much more trouble than usual. I remarked to her that since it was a convenient time during the month for an examination of this kind, we should just as well conduct it."

"She was complaining of considerable pain and tenderness throughout the beginning of the examination," Wynekoop said.

It was at this time that the initial problem began according to Dr. Alice Wynekoop. Alice stated that she suggested some Chloroform be used to make the exam go easier. Dr. Wynekoop then prepared a Chloroform solution that Rheta self-administered using a medicinal sponge.

"She took several deep, slow inhalations of the sponge," Wynekoop said. "I continued my exam and asked her if I was hurting her. She gave no answer."

Dr. Alice Wynekoop continued with her confession. She admitted that when Rheta failed to provide any sort of answer after the Chloroform had been given, she examined her at once. She determined that her breathing had stopped. She administered CPR and artificial respiration techniques immediately for roughly 20 minutes, with no success. Alice Wynekoop examined her fully with a stethoscope, and no heartbeat was revealed. For all intents and purposes, she was officially dead at this point.

The next part of the confession is where things get extremely complicated. At this point in the confession, investigators tend to think that this could be a reasonable instance of doctor error. Assuming what she was confessing at this point were true, she could realistically have been charged with negligent manslaughter. It was what she would continue on to say that baffled investigators and opened the door for conspiracy theories by many.

"I wondered what action could best ease the situation for everyone involved," Dr. Alice Wynekoop went on to confess. "The presence of a loaded revolver seemed to offer the answers that I was seeking. Further injury was now impossible. With great difficulty, I exploded one cartridge at a distance of some half dozen inches from the patient. The gun dropped from my hand."

"The scene was so overwhelming. No action was possible for a period of several hours," She continued.

With this confession, police had all of the evidence that they needed to charge and convict their prime suspect of first-degree murder. Prosecutors were able to use this third statement as confession and admit it to the court room during trial. Although there were many questions that were unanswered, the jury quickly found Dr. Alice Wynekoop guilty of first-degree murder. She was sentenced to 25 years in prison. Being as how she was 62 years old at the time of conviction, this sentence basically was a life sentence.

Assuming that the confession given by Dr. Alice Wynekoop were true, it left a mess of unanswered questions that the defense team tried to use in the court room.

The most pressing question was an obvious one. Alice Wynekoop admitted to firing the shot that killed Rheta Wynekoop. The issue with this is, however, is that she admitted to only one shot. There were three displaced cartridges at the murder scene. The mystery surrounding the other two shots has long been unsolved, as only one bullet was confirmed to have entered into Rheta's body. Many suggest that perhaps Dr. Alice Wynekoop was set to commit suicide, but couldn't keep the gun nestled out of fear. This is just a theory obviously, but no real answer has ever come about.

When police initially came to discover the body of Rheta Wynekoop, it was noted that she had significant amounts of bruising on her body. The bruising was not isolated to one spot. There was discoloration noted on numerous parts of her body. Along with bruising and discoloration were scratches. There were several noticeable scratches to her face and neck area. There wasn't a single part of Dr. Alice Wynekoop's confession that explained these marks. There was no part of the confession that talked of even the slightest struggle. This has long led many to speculate that Rheta was never murdered in the operatory room. A wide belief by many is that the murder happened elsewhere outside of the home. Chloroform was used to make her lose consciousness and she was later shot to finish the job. The bruising and scratches would be evidence that there was a struggle to get her to inhale the Chloroform. The further bruising would show signs of the unconscious body being moved from several locations. This has widely been an accepted theory, especially by those who believe that Earle Wynekoop was really the murderer.

Many wondered what would push an otherwise rational, humanely practicing doctor to commit such a heartless, inhumane act. Police admittedly were shocked at the confession and wondered how she could have gotten to this point. Perhaps the most widely accepted conspiracy theory that has come about with this case is the mother-son conspiracy. This theory is based off of the thought that Dr. Alice Wynekoop could not have possibly committed such a heinous crime. This theory goes into detail about how Earle Wynekoop was stuck in a marriage that was only bringing him misery. Earle also was vastly unsuccessful and freeloading off of his mother. After pressure from both Rheta and his mother, he was at his end with the pressure of it all.

The theory goes to say that Earle Wynekoop shot Rheta Wynekoop in the back outside of the home. He then loaded her body into his car and took her to the Wynekoop home. Upon getting the body into the operatory room, Dr. Alice Wynekoop determined her to be dead. Alice

Wynekoop had an unbreakable love for her son. She quickly came up with a plan to take blame for the murder so that her son would not get in trouble. Earle Wynekoop was then told by Alice to get in the car and start driving before she called to notify police. This would give him an alibi. It was now that she tried to frame herself for the murder and planned her story.

While there are several details added and taken away depending on who you are hearing this theory from, the basis of it is a simple concept. In criminal history, this sort of murder that the theory suggest is quite common. Essentially, a husband or wife wants out of a marriage. To them, murder is an option to get out of the marriage and save reputation and money.

To take this theory even a bit further, many suggest that perhaps Earle and Alice even planned the murder. This is how some explain Dr. Alice Wynekoop taking out the life insurance policy on Rheta for $12,000. While the defense team argues that this is merely a coincidence, it is hard to ignore the timing of that with the murder.

Yet another detail from the confession that didn't make any sense to investigators was the cause of death. Dr. Alice Wynekoop confessed that the Chloroform was what, in fact, killed Rheta Wynekoop. She admitted that she shot Rheta in the back only after she was dead in an effort to perhaps escape persecution. This in itself doesn't make much sense, but when this is coupled with the coroner's report, is just plain false. The blood found in the thorax of Rheta Wynekoop proves that she was alive when she was shot in the back. This is another red flag that many see as more evidence that points to Alice Wynekoop making up a story to cover for someone.

There has also been shaky evidence of the exact whereabouts of Earle Wynekoop on the day of the murder. While Alice Wynekoop stated that he had left on Sunday for his business trip to Arizona, it was confirmed by Stanley Young of Chicago, a nephew of E. Q. Johnson, former United States District Attorney, that Earle and Alice

Wynekoop had a secret meeting on Tuesday morning at 8:00 A.M. This is considered highly odd in any circumstance. Moreover, it is incredibly suspicious that Earle Wynekoop was emphatic about not notifying Rheta that he was still in Chicago.

Stanley Young confirmed that Earle was in Chicago on the day of the murder. While Earle would soon be on the road on the day of the murder, this makes it entirely feasible that something could have happened that morning and he left town to gain an alibi by the time the crime was reported.

Throughout this entire case, police felt like things just didn't add up. Initially, they felt like they had their suspect in Dr. Alice Wynekoop. When Alice Wynekoop ultimately confessed to the entire thing, things still just didn't quite add up to all involved.

Typically, an investigation is centered on the testimony of a suspect who is trying to prove their innocence. The suspect will contort the truth and tell a fabricated statement in a way that will prove they had nothing to do with the crime. Most often, these false statements are quickly picked through by investigators and the truth comes to the surface based on hard evidence and the work of many. This case, however, seems like the opposite happened. Years later, it became more apparent that Dr. Alice Wynekoop was likely not the murderer of Rheta Wynekoop. The puzzling part of the entire case though is that she seemingly lied and fabricated a story in an effort to be found guilty. While everyone could see the obvious flaw in her testimony, she put herself in a position to be found guilty. Whatever really happened on November 21, 1933 in that Chicago neighborhood will never actually be known. This will always be remembered as a case that found the guilty seemingly lying to go to jail.

The Crimes of The Papin Sisters

Amy Delaney

The Papin Sisters

Clémence Derré did not have the best reputation. She was well known for being promiscuous and was not a desirable candidate for Gustave Papin, whose parents disliked the girl, especially after finding out about her affair with her boss. She was the talk of the town, but Gustave was in love, and nothing anybody else could say or do would change his mind. Besides which, Clémence was pregnant with Gustave's baby, and Gustave wanted to do the right thing.

On October 3rd, 1901, Gustave Papin and Clémence Derré were married, and four months later on February 12th, 1902, their daughter Emilia was born.

However, things did not go the way Gustave had imagined. His young wife had absolutely no interest in either her new daughter, or in fact, her husband, and showed little affection to either.

Gustave's suspicions began to grow. Having steadfastly stood by Clémence when the town people had turned against her, he now began to believe that maybe the rumours had been true after all. He started to wonder if it was possible that his wife had not only had an affair with her boss but was still doing so.

Gustave made several attempts to catch his wife out – lying in wait whenever and wherever he thought they might be, but his efforts proved futile.

With his jealousy growing, Gustave decided that the only solution would be to move his wife and daughter away from the town altogether, taking Clémence out of temptation's way.

Gustave set about turning his plans into reality, and in July 1904 he secured himself a position at a saw mill in Marigné, 8km away, believing it to be a second chance for the couple. However, Clémence was furious – she had no desire to leave her home or her lover and reacted by threatening suicide. But by this time she was pregnant with the couple's second child, so she resigned herself to starting a new life in a new village, knowing that nobody else would want a pregnant woman.

On March 8th, 1905, their second child was born – another little girl whom they named Christine. But if Gustave was hoping for a reversal of the state of their marriage he was disappointed, as the relationship disintegrated even further.

Married life was not how Gustave imagined it to be – his wife complained bitterly about her constant tiredness and her unwillingness to look after their daughters, so Gustave took matters into his own hands, and sent Christine to live with his elder sister Isabelle, who also lived in Marigné.

In August 1910 Gustave and Clémence settled in Le Mans with their daughter Emilia, and on September 15th, 1911 Clémence gave birth again, to a third daughter whom they named Léa.[1]

Christine

Christine was happy at her Aunt Isabelle's. Isabelle had a deep mistrust of men but had always wanted to be a mother, so when she was given the opportunity to take in a baby to raise as her own, she jumped at the chance. Isabelle's own mother had been destroyed, at least in Isabelle's eyes, by numerous pregnancies, and she was adamant she was not going to go the same way. She had worked as a maid and when her elderly employer died, Isabelle was left a small inheritance. She was fiercely independent and greatly disapproved of Christine's mother for her various involvements with men. According to Isabelle, as long as a woman stayed away from men she would be safe.

But Christine absorbed her Aunt's hatred of men, and in turn developed her own distrust of them.

Rape

Sometime around Léa's birth, a shocking secret emerged. Clémence found out that her husband, Gustave, had raped their first born daughter, Emilia, who would have been only around ten at the time. Clémence reacted with fury, but she not only directed that fury at her husband but also at her daughter Emilia, whom Clémence believed had seduced Gustave. There was talk of Emilia not being Gustave's daughter, and Clémence assumed that the little girl had been a willing sexual partner to her father, and had enjoyed it.

Clémence took her revenge on both of them.

She divorced Gustave, as one would expect for such a heinous crime, but she also took revenge on Emilia, sending her away to a religious orphanage called Le Bon Pasteur. The orphanage had a reputation for harshness, and Clémence thought it might force her 'errant' daughter to mend her ways. At the same time, Clémence removed Christine from Isabelle's care and placed her alongside her sister at the orphanage. Baby Léa was given to a great-uncle to be looked after, and Clémence, now both husband and child free, obtained work as a maid.[2]

Léa

Léa stayed with her uncle until 1918, when she was around seven. When her uncle died, Clémence placed Léa into a religious institution in Le Mans[3], where she would stay until 1924.

Emilia

Not a lot is known about Emilia Papin, except that, after her time at Le Bon Pasteur, she decided to enter the convent and dedicate her life to the church. As far as records show, she spent the rest of her life there.[4]

Back to Christine

Christine was set to follow in her older sister's footsteps – she, too, wanted to join a convent. While she had had Emilia at Le Bon Pasteur with her, she had felt protected and loved, but with Emilia now in a convent, Christine found herself alone. The love she had felt for Emilia now had nowhere to go, as entering the convent no doubt meant excommunicating herself from her family. So Christine turned her affections towards her little sister, Léa.

Christine's plans were scuppered by Clémence, however. The woman had been furious when Emilia had joined the convent, as she had been getting to an age when she could go out to work and earn money to send to her mother. So when Christine decided she wanted the same life, Clémence put her foot down, exercising her parental rights.[5]

At that time, in France, the age of majority was 21, meaning that parents had the deciding say on what their children did up until that time. So Clémence, seeing her meal ticket disappearing the same way it had with Emilia, prevented Christine from joining a convent and instead committed her to a life of service.

Christine was well suited to the life of a maid – she had spent eight years at Le Bon Pasteur where she had been expertly taught in skills such as housekeeping and sewing.

Christine found work easily enough, but she was forced to leave several jobs because, according to her mother, the pay wasn't enough for her (Clémence's) needs.

When Léa was old enough, she too went into service, and the two sisters often worked together in the various homes of their employers.

The Lancelins

In 1926, when Christine was 22, she managed to secure a position with the Lancelin family in Le Mans.

René Lancelin was a retired lawyer, who lived at No. 6 rue Bruyère, with his wife, Léonie, and their grown-up daughter, Geneviève. The couple had another daughter who lived away from home.

When Christine had been working for the Lancelins for two months, she asked them if they would consider hiring Léa as well. Madame Lancelin was impressed with the standard of Christine's work, so she agreed to take on her younger sister too.

Life went on, with Christine working as the cook and Léa as the chambermaid. The girls were diligent with their work, putting in 12-14 hour days and working six and a half days a week. Their only time off was a half day on Sundays when the girls would attend church, dressed appropriately, with gloves and hats.

The sisters had no interests outside of each other and the church, apart from an occasional visit to a local medium, and the remainder of their time was spent in the attic room they shared. They showed no interest in meeting suitors, or dancing, or going to the movies.[6]

At first, it would seem that the sisters had a reasonable relationship with Madame Lancelin. When their employer found out that they were sending their wages to their mother, Clémence, she urged them to stop passing it on and keep it for themselves. She even went so far as to tell Clémence herself that her 'gravy train' had now stopped. The girls' wages were around 3000 francs per year, which amounts to around $2236 today.[7]

Because of Madame Lancelin's kindness, the sisters began referring to her as 'Maman' in private.

Although their living arrangements were basic – the sisters shared one small bed in the attic for instance – they had a balcony from which they could watch the people of Le Mans pass by. It was a relative luxury among the serving community.[8] Indeed, as servants go, the sisters had it better than most. There was always plenty to eat, and the girls had a heated bedroom, a luxury which many other servants of the time were denied.

The Tide Turns

After a few years, things began to take a downward turn in the Lancelin household. Although both the girls had an enviable reputation with regards to their work, their personalities seemed to cause some consternation among other people. Local shopkeepers found the girls to be aloof and reserved, and one woman, who herself had employed Christine for a couple of weeks, described her time with Christine as difficult, stating that she found the girl so touchy and rebellious that she was loath to ask her to do anything. Nonetheless, their professional standing was second to none – unlike other maids of the time, the sisters did not engage in any flirtations with local boys and applied themselves meticulously to their duties.

Despite Madame Lancelin's initial kindness in ensuring the girls got to keep their wages, she became an increasingly hard taskmaster and took to wearing white gloves to check that the sisters had left no dust anywhere.

Communication became stinted. Madame Lancelin would only communicate with Christine and not Léa, and even then it would invariably be via a typed message regarding their work rather than through actual conversation.

Monsieur Lancelin himself later admitted that he had never once spoken to Christine or Léa during their seven years of service in his house.[9]

Sisterly Love

The fact that the sisters spent so much time together alone in their room did not go unnoticed. Christine was also fiercely protective of Léa, and was apparently extremely jealous of Genevieve Lancelin, whenever she attempted to initiate conversation with the younger sister. On one of the girls' visits to the local medium, they had apparently been told that Christine had been Léa's husband in a past life, a belief which she seemed to act out. In fact, such was the abnormality of the closeness and affection the sisters shared for each other that Madame Lancelin and her family began to suspect that the two young women were engaged in sexual relations.[10]

The sisters were unnaturally close, described by some that knew them as obsessive. They would braid each other's hair, make clothes for each other, and spent every moment together, completely shunning any outside interests. On one occasion, Madame Lancelin took it upon herself to spy on the women and had her suspicions confirmed when she caught the sisters making love. One can only imagine the shock – at the time homosexuality was very much frowned upon, and when you add incest to the mix it became even more scandalous. To the girls, though, their behaviour probably felt completely normal. Their own father had raped their sister, and their Aunt had consistently warned against the perils of mixing with men.[11] Their father had disappeared from their lives after his sexual abuse of Emelia had come out, apparently fighting in World War One and subsequently re-marrying[12]) and they had found in each other the affection and love that their own mother had been unwilling or unable to provide. The love they had for each other was the only love they had ever truly known. Madame Lancelin decided to share what she had seen with the rest of her family, but for one reason or another no action was taken, and life carried on.

The situation became more strained after a particular incident involving Léa and Madame Lancelin. While cleaning the floor, Léa had missed a tiny scrap of paper, which Madame Lancelin noticed, and, enraged by the girl's inattention to detail, pinched Léa hard and viciously until she was forced to her knees to pick up the offending piece of paper. Léa, who was normally very quiet and withdrawn, told Christine *"She had better not try that again or I will defend myself."*[13]

Christine's Descent into Madness

Towards the end of 1932, Christine's behaviour began to change. She began to suffer explosive fits of anger which she directed at her younger sister, Léa. The previously loving, albeit unnatural, relationship became a frightening ordeal for the younger sister as she could do nothing but suffer her older sister's outbursts which came from nowhere. Her normally kind demeanour was slowly changing into that of someone totally alien to her.

The pair continued to perform their duties for the Lancelin family, but Christine was losing her grip on reality. She began to suffer from hallucinations – seeing and hearing things which were not there, and these episodes, which today would have been recognized as symptoms of paranoid schizophrenia, in turn, set off panic attacks in Léa, who could not cope with her sister's state of mind, and behaviour.

It was all about to come to a tragic and fatal head.

February 2nd, 1933

The late winter was making its presence felt in Le Mans on February 2nd, 1933. It was bitterly cold, and the wind was howling outside.[14] Madame Lancelin had spent the day shopping with her daughter, Genevieve, and the pair were due to meet Monsieur Lancelin at his brother in law's house for dinner later that evening. Christine and Léa were not expecting their employer home until late into the night.

One of Léa's jobs for that day had been to take a broken iron to the electrician's to be fixed. However, when she returned home and plugged it in ready to do some ironing, it shorted the power to the entire house. As the Lancelins weren't due home until late that night, Christine took the decision to leave fixing the fuse until the next morning.

However, Madame and Genevieve Lancelin did return home, sometime after 5.30 pm, and were annoyed to find the house in darkness. Christine met them at the door and explained that the iron had been fixed, but that when it had been plugged in it had shorted the power. Madame Lancelin was furious at this news and a row broke out.

It was enough to tip Christine over the edge.

The older sister grabbed a pewter jug and brought it down onto Madame Lancelin's head. Her daughter, Genevieve, heard the commotion and came rushing to her mother's aid, only to receive a similar blow. As Christine began to fight with Genevieve, Léa joined in, struggling with Madame Lancelin, who had managed to recover somewhat from the blow. As the fight continued in the darkness, Christine shouted: *"I'm going to massacre them."*

As the fight became more frenzied, Christine began to shout orders to her sister.

"Smash her head into the ground" and "tear her eyes out"!

Léa had always followed her older sister's orders, and she wasn't about to stop now. With her bare hands, she gouged Madame Lancelin's eyes out, while Christine did the same thing to Genevieve.

As the two women lay writhing, blind and in agony on the floor, the sisters went on the search for weapons with which to continue their brutal attack. Finding a knife and a hammer, they returned to the grisly scene, and systematically beat their employers with first the pewter jug, and then the hammer. Mercifully for the Lancelin women, death came at last. But, even though they could no longer feel it, their mutilation was far from over.

The Papin sisters then 'prepared' the bodies of the two women as if they were preparing a joint of meat for dinner, carving deep gashes into their flesh. Lifting the skirts of the two women over their heads, leaving them with no dignity whatsoever, the maids sliced into their thighs and buttocks. Their final act of humiliation was to smear Madame Lancelin's body with Genevieve's menstrual blood, basting her as they would baste a joint of beef.

The Discovery

While his wife and daughter were being slaughtered in their own home, Monsieur Lancelin was at first irritated, and then worried, when they failed to show up for dinner. He made the journey home to pick them up, but when he arrived he couldn't get in. The house was locked and bolted from the inside. He thought it strange that the maids hadn't answered the door, but decided that perhaps they hadn't heard him and that his wife and daughter had already left for Madame Lancelin's brother's house.

When he returned to his brother in law's house, however, there was still no sign of his wife or daughter, and Monsieur Lancelin began to worry. Enlisting the help of a dinner guest, he returned once more to his house, but he still could not get inside. Furthermore, the house was in darkness apart from a candle flickering in the window of the maids' attic bedroom.

Finally, he went to the police with his concerns.

One of the policemen who returned to the house with Monsieur Lancelin climbed the wall at the back of the house and gained entry through the kitchen door.

As he cautiously made his way through the house, his path lit only by his flashlight, the policeman could see no signs of a struggle. Everything was in place, giving no clues as to what had happened.

But as he climbed the stairs to the second floor, the beam of light fell on an object on the floor. Small, and round. At first, the policeman couldn't tell what it was, but as he looked closer, he realized to his horror that it was an eyeball.

It became clear to the policeman that more horrors were to come, and he called down to Monsieur Lancelin not to come any further into the house.

As he continued to climb the stairs, the officer stumbled upon the bodies of Madame and Genevieve Lancelin. Or rather, he assumed it was them, as their faces had been smashed with such ferocity that they were unrecognizable. Both women had had their eyes removed, and Madame Lancelin's eyeballs were discovered in the folds of the scarf she was wearing.

The officers were aware that in addition to the Lancelins, there were two maids living in the house. Assuming the bodies they had just discovered had been slaughtered by a madman, they climbed the second flight of stairs to the attic, fearing that they would also find the mutilated bodies of Christine and Léa. They were also mindful of the fact that the murderer, or murderers, might still be in the house.

The door to the maids' room was locked from the inside, and the gendarme could see candlelight flickering from within. Calls to the girls to open the door were futile, so the officers broke down the door, and entered the small attic room.

Christine and Léa Papin were huddled up in bed together, having carefully removed their blood stained clothes and washed their bodies, before putting on clean bedclothes and climbing into bed together.

Next to the bed was a blood soaked hammer.[15]

What Happened Next

The sisters were taken for questioning. Christine was unapologetic in her admission of guilt, explaining matter-of-factly what had happened when the Lancelin women had returned home. Describing the moment that Madame Lancelin lost her temper over the iron, Christine continued:

"Then I rushed down to the kitchen and went to fetch a hammer and a knife, and with both instruments my sister and I fought on our two mistresses, we stabbed [their] heads with a knife, Struck with a pot of tin which was placed on a small table on the landing. We changed the instruments several times from one to the other, that is to say, that I passed to my sister the Hammer to strike and she passed the knife to us, we did the same with the tin pot, and the victims screamed, but I do not remember that they spoke a few words. I went to lock the door and closed the door of the vestibule as well. I closed these doors because I liked it better than the police who noticed our crime before our boss. Then my sister and I went to wash our hands...because we had them full of blood, then we got into our room, we took off our belongings which were stained with blood, we put on a bathrobe, we closed the door to our room, and we went to bed Both in the same bed. This is where you found us when you broke the door. I do not have any regrets or, in other words, I cannot tell you if I do not have any, I prefer to have the skin of my bosses rather than that they have mine or that of my sister. I did not premeditate my crime, I had no hatred towards them, but I do not accept the gesture that Madame Lancelin had for me this evening."

Léa refused to give any account of the evening's events, only to say that she agreed with everything Christine had said, adding:

"Everything [my] sister told you is accurate, the crimes happened exactly as she told you. My role in this case is absolutely the one she told you. I struck as much as she did, and I assert that we had not premeditated to kill our patrons, the idea came to us instantly when we heard that

Madame Lancelin reproached us. [Like] my sister I have no regret for the criminal act we have committed...like my sister, I prefer to have the skin of my bosses rather than those who have had our own."[16]

The Trial

The Papin sisters were brought to trial in September 1933. It was an event which was followed by people all over France, and police had to be drafted in to help control the crowds.

In the run-up to the trial, Christine's behavior became more and more disturbing. The sisters had been separated after their arrest, and Christine displayed sexually driven behavior, calling out for her sister and writhing around on the floor in a sexual manner. She also began to experience the same hallucinations she had while she was with the Lancelins, and on one occasion attempted to gouge her own eyes out, resulting in her being restrained in a straight jacket.

Following this incident, Christine recanted her statement, claiming responsibility for both murders, and saying that Léa had had nothing to do with either of them. Léa, however, continued to take responsibility for her part, and Christine's attempts to free her sister were dismissed at the trial.

The sisters were both found guilty of murder. Christine was sentenced to death by guillotine, while Léa, who had only been charged with the murder of Madame Lancelin, received a lighter sentence of ten years' hard labor, as the jury believed that she had been heavily influenced by her older sister.

Christine's sentence was later commuted to life imprisonment, but she did not fare well. Pining for her beloved Léa, Christine became deeply depressed and stopped eating. She was transferred to an asylum in Rennes, but her condition never improved and she died in 1937 of *cachexia* – literally wasting away.

Léa, on the other hand, fared much better. She kept her head down and did what was asked of her, and after eight years she was released on good behavior. Extraordinarily, she settled in Nantes with her mother,

Clémence, where she assumed the name of Marie and gained employment as a chambermaid.[17]

Léa

In September 1966, an article ran in the newspaper *France-Soir*. A journalist had tracked Léa down and interviewed her. Although the article was factually incorrect, and somewhat moralizing, it gave readers a glimpse into the madness that had taken hold of the youngest Papin sister.

"I do what I can to keep my room simple so that my sister, who watches me from above (because I'm certain she is in Paradise), doesn't laugh at me. I pray for her. I pray for our mother who lived with me until she died. To help me, she said...and all at once I didn't pray anymore. Christine watches me. She is always beautiful and young. She smiles as in the old days: with irony! I come apart, I shrivel up, I sweat from fear, I faint...And there's a trunk in my room."

She talked about her work at the hotel, and the fear she felt every time she made a mistake - of the young chambermaids who worked with her, and the teasing they bestowed upon her.

But her last words to the journalist showed her lack of grasp on reality and the sad delusion she had created for herself.

"When I don't have to work anymore, I want to become Sister Marie, at Bon Pasteur, in Le Mans. I've been saving for it. At Bon Pasteur, one of my older sisters is a nun. I'll go back to her..."[18]

HUSBAND KILLER SHARI TOBYNE

ANA BENSON

When it comes to female killers, the most common type of crime is mariticide or murdering their husbands. There are many motivations behind taking someone's life but killing a person so close to you is often fueled by passion, financial gain, jealousy, or betrayal. The case of Shari Tobyne is the perfect example of a woman scorned. Her husband of thirty-five years wanted to divorce her due to the financial problems she caused by mishandling the couple's finances.

So one day before he was set to leave their rented house and move on, Shari snapped. She simply couldn't allow him to leave after so many years they spend together. Shari continued to live her life normally, but Arizona police started uncovering body parts from counties surrounding the city of Phoenix and they couldn't determine the exact identity of the deceased man. Worried Tobyne children alerted the law enforcement that their father was missing and this is where the story started to unravel.

It will soon be discovered that a loving mother and a grandmother murdered her husband in cold blood because leaving him was simply not an option.

Early life

Shari Tobyne was born on 24th of July, 1956 in Clifton, Kansas. She grew up in a rural area just outside of the city. Her parents owned a farm and her father was quite successful in his line of business. She was a happy, carefree girl who enjoyed spending time in nature and would often help her family by jumping in and completing difficult farm related tasks.

This is where she met her future husband, Dwight Tobyne. He lived just across the street from Shari and his parents ran their own agricultural business. Dwight loved Shari's personality and energy so he soon realized that he had a crush on her. However, he didn't want to make a move too quickly so he waited until he got a college acceptance letter to ask Shari to be his girlfriend. She was still in high school at that time.

Both Shari and Dwight wanted to achieve business success and escape their small town. They soon realized that they were a match made in heaven because they cheered each other on and offered great support when needed. The couple married in 1975 and they made a decision to move to Salina, Kansas to start their life as a husband and wife. They wanted to make a better future for their family and relocating to a big city was their best option.

Shari was a bit apprehensive at first but the fact that she had Dwight right there beside her made the transition a lot easier. Dwight started a semester at the University of Kansas, studying Animal Sciences while Shari wanted to be a perfect wife and keep their home in pristine conditions. The pressure was on Dwight and he simply had to succeed with his academic work because he was supposed to carry the Tobyne family to the business success eventually.

The couple's first child, Jennifer was born in 1977. They welcomed a baby boy, Brad only three years later. The family was growing but Dwight was still in college, trying to graduate. Shari was very stressed about the financial situation and they struggled to take care of their children. Dwight did his best to earn some extra money so he landed a part-time job in hopes it would cover the expenses.

Trading stocks and interests were all the rage back in the 1980s and Dwight though it would be a perfect opportunity to invest the money he had on his account and try his luck. It wasn't his field of study and he soon got lost in all the numbers and investment opportunities. He pretty much gambled away all of their family savings and they ended up getting evicted from their townhouse. They packed their things and moved back to their parents.

With a third child on its way, the Tobyne family was under a lot of stress. Dwight even though about leaving Shari because he felt like he had failed both her and their children. Being the provider was already very hard for him and the fact that he managed to spend all of their money created additional pressure. Moving back to their parents was another blow. The situation was dismal and both of them knew that they have to make some difficult decisions in near future.

The move and success

The Tobyne family wanted to have a new beginning so they packed their things and moved to Denver, Colorado. Dwight was ecstatic because he can continue his education up there and earn a master's degree that will certainly come in handy when it comes to finding employment in near future. He also landed a full-time job at a bank and the pay was quite good.

Inspired by the economic boom of the 1990s, Dwight Tobyne enrolled into a business school and earned a diploma after a couple of years. Combining everything he learned with smart ideas and investments, Dwight created a leasing company. It was exactly what Denver needed at the time and he knew it would be a success.

It took Dwight a few years to make some serious money and now the family was living comfortably in a large house. They had everything imaginable and Shari finally started to feel confident. She knew that Dwight was a hard worker but she did have doubts when the company was first started because she knew how it felt to lose money.

The Tobynes looked like a perfect family because they were wealthy, active in the community, and their children were successful in school. Shari loved the attention and enjoyed a classy lifestyle that was a complete opposite of the things they went through in Kansas. She felt the need to contribute to the wealth of her family so she got her real estate license. It was time to stop being a housewife and start doing things on her own.

Dwight supported his wife's decision to create her own business and they cheered each other on as usual. They would often collaborate and help each other out with work-related tasks. Everything seemed to go really well for the Tobynes and they continued to live large with their ever-growing wealth.

The first sign of trouble

In 2003, Shari and Dwight lived alone in their family house. The children have moved out and the two of them still ran their business successfully. One day, Shari told Dwight that she made some mistakes regarding one of her accounts and that the numbers were not adding up. Her client lost their money due to this mistake and Shari's real estate license was taken away. Her job and the real estate career were in jeopardy.

It was clear that Shari tried to commit some type of fraud but she was never prosecuted for that. The Tobynes had plenty of money left in the bank and since they were experts at the new beginnings, they thought it would be the perfect time to move somewhere warmer. Dwight told his friends that they were going to Arizona because the real estate opportunities down there are amazing. But the truth was they were fleeing the city because the majority of their neighbors were aware of Shari's bad business decisions and they needed to surround themselves with people who don't know them well.

They bought a huge house in Gilbert, Arizona which was as posh and classy as their previous residence. It was a part of a gated community outside of Phoenix and they felt right at home. Dwight continued with his leasing business and it seemed like Phoenix was really a good relocation choice because he was getting a lot of work there. Since Shari was not employed, she became very involved with the way Dwight ran his business. She started helping him out because she had plenty of free time on her hands. Shari was in charge of family finances.

But in 2008, Dwight started getting phone calls from his friends and clients who were asking about his health. The majority of them though that he was in a hospital. Dwight figured out that Shari was behind this and that she was telling them that he had a heart-attack. He got really worried and started going through his company's financial records. He noticed something alarming – he was missing a large amount of money and since Shari was in charge of the accounts, he asked her about it.

The confrontation was quite explosive, mostly because Dwight couldn't believe that she could do something like that to him. After all, they have been married for decades and stealing from his own company was simply shocking. Shari had an explanation for everything and she told Dwight that she took the money to pay the bills and other necessities. Dwight was still unconvinced and furious. He knew what she had done in Denver and this looked almost the same.

Just a couple of weeks after the fight, Shari contacted her children and she sounded distracted. They weren't sure what was happening but it was clear that something was very wrong. Dwight was at the house when he realized that he hadn't seen his wife for hours. After combing every room of their home, he went out to his neighbor's house and he found Shari laying on a couch. There was an empty pill bottle right beside her. Shari wasn't responding and he called an ambulance.

Once she was conscious, Shari explained that she did try to kill herself because she simply couldn't take it any longer. She hid important information from Dwight and he found everything out in the hospital. They were in serious debt and their accounts were pretty much emptied out. The reality came crashing down on Dwight and he couldn't hide the sadness from his face. His business was ruined and he worked hard for nothing. He was still in disbelief that his own wife could have done this.

The Tobynes had to sell their lavish house in the gated community in order to cover at least a portion of the debt. It was a psychological shock to both of them because they had to find a smaller place to live in. They were back at the square one. So they gathered their things and moved to Scottsdale, Arizona.

The tensions between the pair were high and Dwight was on the fence about divorcing Shari. He made a decision to leave her in autumn of 2009 because he couldn't forget the things she put him through.

However, they did their best to appear as normal as possible in front of their children. But when Dwight failed to show up at the Thanksgiving dinner in November of 2009, Shari confessed that Dwight left her and moved to Mexico. None of their children could have predicted that Shari was not telling the truth about the divorce and that the reality was more sinister.

The murder of Dwight Tobyne

In November of 2009, Shari bought herself a gun. She started practicing shooting at a local gun range and her last visit to that place was on 22nd of November. It looked like the divorce was the final straw that made her think about murdering her own husband. After getting a sense of how the gun worked, all she needed to do is find the right time to shoot Dwight. The exact date of the murder is still unknown but sometime between 24th and 28th of November 2009, Shari entered the couple's bedroom and fired the gun at Dwight Tobyne. It is presumed that she shot him in the head.

She then wrapped his lifeless body into the carpet that was already soaking up the blood and dragged him to a garage where she proceeded to chop his corpse into pieces. She took her time with each and every part, first cutting off the arms and feet. She did use a saw, as well as some other tools, but Shari also tore away some pieces herself. The garage was a mess and she needed to get rid of every single evidence that could connect her to the murder.

After wrapping the parts into cellophane and carpet cutouts, she loaded them up in her car and started making rounds through adjacent counties, dropping them in remote areas by an interstate. She did her best to leave them a bit away from the road in hopes that the animals would drag the parts even further into the wilderness. She was certain that this was the way to keep the police off her trail and ensure that she will not get caught. She then cleaned the crime scene with plenty of bleach, removing each and every spec of blood from the floor and walls. She presumably got rid of the saw and other tools as well.

She kept Dwight's cell phone and intended to pretend like he simply left her. She planned to contact her children every now and then via text messages and e-mails so they would think that Dwight was alive and well, soaking up the sun in Mexico. Since Shari wouldn't make any profit from her husband's death, the only explanation was that this was a crime of passion. They were married for almost thirty-five years and Dwight simply couldn't leave her right then after everything they went through. Shari's emotions obviously get the best of her and the result was gruesome.

The discovery of the crime

Even though Dwight missed the Thanksgiving dinner, the biggest red flag was the fact that he wasn't present at the birth of the Tobyne's second grandchild. He did contact his children via text messages so they though he was alive and well. But when he didn't show up at the hospital, his oldest daughter alerted the police. It was July of 2010 and the law enforcement immediately started working on this case.

The Tobyne children told the authorities that their father wanted to move to Oklahoma but their mother told them that he went to Mexico. The investigators were certain that the story was false so they focused their attention on Shari since she was the last known person to see him alive. She was living with her children at the time because she had to move out from the condo she shared with her husband and didn't have enough money to support herself on her own. When they brought Shari for the first interview, she denied everything. Shari told them that she had no idea where her husband was at the moment and that he hadn't contacted her in months.

She was released but the police investigators did sense that something was very wrong with her statements. They decided to put her under surveillance in order to see what she would do next and monitor any possible suspicious activities. Just like it was expected, Shari started acting oddly. The police officers saw her disposing of something in a dumpster and when they got there, they discovered a couple of clothing items, as well as pieces of a gun. She then proceeded to clean the trunk of her car which was even more alarming to the detectives because it looked like she was getting rid of the possible evidence.

Then they managed to locate Dwight's Ford pickup truck at a parking lot. It was obvious that the car was there for months but no one had reported it because it was parked in front of a residential building and there were a lot of vehicles there on a daily basis. There was no physical evidence of the crime anywhere in the car which meant that Shari probably didn't use it for body disposal. Checking the cell phone records was the next step and the investigators discovered that both of their phones were at the same location during the time frame when the possible murder occurred, as well as afterward. So Shari's story about Dwight leaving for Mexico in November of 2009 was clearly false because he wouldn't leave his phone behind. It was time to bring her back to the station for a second interview.

Shari broke down under pressure and told the detectives a whole new story. She said that she bought the gun with an intention to use in for her own suicide. Shari was feeling horrible after everything she had done with her husband's money and she wanted to end her life. The fact that Dwight was leaving her added to her depression and she simply couldn't continue to live anymore.

She brought the gun to their bedroom wanting to shoot herself in the head. Instead, Dwight who was there as well noticed the gun, grabbed it from her hands and unintentionally pulled the trigger while they were fighting for the weapon. He shot himself and was losing a lot of blood quickly. He was soon dead. Shari then said that she was lost and scared, knowing that no one would believe her story. So she quickly wrapped her husband in the sheets and dragged him to her car. She drove off to a remote location and left his body there.

Shari insisted that the death was an accident and that she didn't mean to hurt her husband. She volunteered to take the investigators to the place where she dumped the body. Listening to her directions, they went east of Scottsdale and started combing through the area. They couldn't find any traces of Dwight's corpse even though they covered a wide field around the alleged dump site. They knew that a lot of time has passed since the killing and that animals could have dragged the body someplace else, but they couldn't find anything that could indicate that a corpse was there in the first place.

The investigators placed Shari in the jail and continued to question other possible witnesses that could shed some light on this case. It was obvious that Shari's story was either incomplete or entirely false. They approached the owner of the apartment which Tobyne's were renting at the time of the murder. She told the police that the carpet in the master bedroom was brand new after Shari left the condo and that she also noticed a strong smell of bleach in the garage. It was a minor clue at the time because the investigators knew that Shari was an obsessive cleaner and she would often go around the house with pure bleach in order to disinfect all the surfaces. However, once they put the pieces back together, the bleach will play an important part in the investigation because it was used to clean up the scene.

Finding Dwight Tobyne

Back in December of 2009, prior to the missing person report which was filed by Dwight's children, dismembered body parts were found near a highway in Pinal County, namely legs without feet. The cuts were partially clean but they could see that the murderer did apply some force and they were more focused on tearing off the limbs than on keeping everything pristine. The police officers were sure that a saw of some kind was used in the process. The parts were collected by the police and sent for further analysis. The second set of body parts was discovered in La Paz County only a couple of days later. Hikers bumped onto a man's torso near the main road and alerted the authorities who once again collected the evidence.

Two police departments got into contact and they examined their findings in order to determine that the parts belonged to the same person. And then, three days later, a person traveling on a motorbike noticed something strange on the side of the road near Sugarloaf exit. The authorities in the area were already aware that they had a dismembered body on their hands and the remains were transported to Pinal County to make sure they also came from the same victim. The results were positive but the identity of the man was still unknown because they hadn't found the hands so fingerprint search was out of the question. As a matter of fact, some remains are still missing to this day.

The investigators who were working on Dwight Tobyne's case were aware of the mystery man who was found in three counties and they took a DNA swab from his parents in order to see if it was the match. The dates of the discoveries overlapped their murder theory and the detectives feared the worst. But before they delivered it to the medical examiner's office, they compared Dwight's physical description with the collected body parts. Hugh Lockerby, a detective from Scottsdale who worked on this case said: "A left leg was recovered first. A couple of days later, north of Phoenix, right leg was discovered. One hundred miles west of Phoenix a complete torso was uncovered. I asked could they give me a little description of the race, the height, the weight, and I am listening as they are telling me this and that is the exact description of Dwight Tobyne."

When the tests came back positive, they confirmed that it was, in fact, Dwight Tobyne. Since Shari Tobyne didn't mention any dismemberment of the body in her second statement, they had enough evidence to prove that she was lying. It was time to confront her and try to find out what exactly happened on that fatal night in November of 2009.

Shari pleaded not guilty in front of a judge and repeated her story about the accidental shooting. Her lawyer, Anne Phillips asked the judge to allow a psychological evaluation of her client because she was impossible to communicate with. She refused to provide her with any helpful details and Phillips thought that Shari might need some psychological help due to the fact that she was suicidal in the past.

Her attorney also wanted to be sure that Shari Tobyne did understand the charges properly. It looked like she was not fully there and her responses were sparse, providing Phillips with short answers only. The judge allowed a psychiatric examination and it was confirmed that Shari was responsive and aware of her actions. She didn't suffer from psychosis or depression. There were no underlying psychological issues and she was capable of attending her own trial.

However, the way she acted after the murder told the psychiatrist who conducted the evaluation that Shari Tobyne was a textbook sociopath. Not every person has the ability to separate their emotions and continue acting normally after a crime like this. She was sticking to her story no matter how unlikely it sounded and it seemed like Shari did really believe in her version of the shooting.

The trial

As previously mentioned, Shari Tobyne pleaded not guilty in the initial hearing. The state had a solid case against her even though they had no witnesses to the murder itself. She did confess to accidental shooting so she clearly was involved to some degree. However, her actions after the gun went off told a different story about a very violent body dismemberment and disposal. The fact that Shari lied to the authorities about the location of the body dump added a whole new layer to the case. She obviously didn't want the body to be found and hoped that the animals would do the dirty work for her.

Shari was facing the charges of a first-degree murder, as well as a concealment of the body parts. Since she did have some sketchy history regarding the financial fraud, the authorities had enough evidence to add it to the charges as well. They were asking for the death penalty. Shari's attorney didn't have much to work with but she repeated her old story about the accidental shooting. The verdict could have gone in both ways at that point, depending on the jury. So instead of going on a trial, Shari decided to end it as quickly as possible.

Shari Tobyne pleaded guilty on May 19th, 2012, ending the trial. It was the only way she could avoid the death penalty. That was a clever decision because her claims were simply not strong enough to convince everyone that she didn't shoot her husband on purpose. So instead she received life in prison and an additional thirty-one years for the financial fraud.

The children were in shock from the beginning of this case and they had a difficult time accepting the fact that their loving mother could actually kill their father. Shari Tobyne remains behind the bars and it is unclear when and if she would get an opportunity for an appeal.

ADRIANA VASCO : KILLER FOR HIRE

82

JESSI GILLMAN

"Somebody just assassinated them."

When a security guard discovered a car parked along the shoulder of the Ortega Highway on November 20, 1999, with the engine running and the lights on, he assumed it was a couple of kids making out. Instead, he found the bullet-riddled bodies of a prominent Huntington Beach doctor and his optometrist wife sprawled across the vehicle's front seat.

"The car is running, the lights are on – he walks up to the car and looks through the driver's side window, and he gets a glimpse of a horrific scene," said Michael Fleeman, who wrote about the murder of Kenneth Stahl and Carolyn Oppy-Stahl in his book, *Deadly Mistress*.

Stahl, 57, and his wife had been out celebrating her 44th birthday the day before when he suddenly pulled over on the side of the road. The couple was about 30 miles from home – driving in the opposite direction. Just two hours later, investigators were digging for clues that would help them solve the murder – with no leads, no obvious motives, and no witnesses.

"When I arrived there, the driver had a gunshot wound near the bridge of his nose," said Jim McDonald, a senior investigator with the Orange County sheriff's department who worked on the case. "It appeared to be an entry wound – it looked like he'd been shot in the face. There was also another entry wound in the upper part of his chest."

McDonald said Stahl was still upright in the driver's seat, with his seatbelt still securely fastened. The passenger, Oppy, was laying down in the car, with her head near the centre console and at least one leg hanging out the open passenger door. McDonald added that she had multiple gunshot wounds to both the front and back of her body.

Investigators quickly ruled out the possibility that the scene was the result of a murder-suicide between the husband and wife, as no gun had been located in the car. There was also no evidence of a robbery, as both victims still had their wallets and plenty of cash when they were discovered.

"It was as if they'd pulled over and somebody just assassinated them," Fleeman said.

The case went unsolved for more than ten months before it was passed off to a new team, Detectives Brian Meaney and Felipe Villalobos. Veterans of the force with a solid, effective partnership, Meaney and Villalobos got to work immediately – reading over old case files, interviewing people, and bouncing around possible theories. Eventually, they made a breakthrough.

"It's a tale of intrigue, a tale of murder," said Orange County Sheriff Mike Carona. "But most importantly, it's a tale of some outstanding police work, some outstanding detective work."

While going through Stahl's cell phone log, the detectives saw the same number pop up with consistent frequency. The number belonged to a medical receptionist named Adriana Vasco, who worked at one of Stahl's clinics. When they interviewed the receptionist, a potential motive began to take shape. Vasco wasn't just the receptionist – she'd been having an affair with Stahl for many years, and he'd been providing her with regular financial support.

This wasn't the first time Stahl had cheated on a spouse. Already twice divorced, Oppy's sister Linda Dubay said Stahl had engaged in a series of affairs. Oppy had considered the possibility of seeking a divorce herself, saddened and angry with her husband's many infidelities, but according to Dubay, she maintained hope that Stahl would change.

"She had put up with so much and got used to it," said Dubay. "Somehow, the unknown is more scary than the known."

No matter how much effort Oppy put into the marriage, Dubay said she received little in return. According to Dubay, Stahl struggled to meet the expectations his family had for him – his father was a well-respected surgeon and CEO of a hospital, while Stahl worked as an anaesthesiologist.

"(Stahl) needed the ego boost of his affairs – usually with divorced nurses, single mothers, needy individuals," Dubay said.

Vasco was a perfect fit.

The black sheep

"She never really knew her father, didn't seem to get along well with her mother," said Fleeman, who heavily researched Vasco's background for his book, *Deadly Mistress*.

Born in Mexico as the product of a rape, Vasco suffered both physical and sexual abuse at the hands of her stepfather before leaving her family's home at the age of 16. The next few years, she "bounced around" the homes of friends and relatives, according to Detective Felipe Villalobos.

"She was like the black sheep of the family," said Deborah Burns, the manager at Vasco's Anaheim apartment. "She used to always say that."

However, Vasco quickly discovered that her looks and sex appeal could get her anything she wanted or needed – but she struggled to find a meaningful relationship. Her history of abuse had also given her "an almost pathologically bad taste in men," said Fleeman.

"She was very, very sexual," he explained. "Her exotic Latin looks attracted many men, and all of them said she was a sexual dynamo – they couldn't get enough of her. But she never had any kind of relationship that lasted very long."

At 25, one of Vasco's failed relationships left her a single mom – but in 1992, her luck started to change when she met Dr. Kenneth Stahl at her new job as a medical receptionist at a pain clinic.

"Stahl was a 57-year old anaesthesiologist that had set up a couple of his own businesses, pain clinics, "said Senior Prosecutor Dennis Conway. "At first, they were just friendly with each other, but then they started sharing details about their personal lives with one another."

Vasco and Stahl bonded over their struggles with intimate relationships. Stahl was excited that a much younger woman was paying him attention, while Vasco was flattered to have a well-established older man interested in more than just her body. After about a year, the pair finally gave in to the undeniable attraction that had formed between them.

"They developed a romantic relationship, and a very passionate sexual relationship," Fleeman said. "(Vasco) gave him, by all accounts, this wild and crazy sex life that he had never had before."

According to Fleeman, Vasco's behaviour with Stahl was consistent with her "pattern" – using sex to manipulate men into doing anything she wanted. By fulfilling his sexual fantasies, it appeared Vasco had Stahl wrapped around her finger.

"Friends of hers that she worked with said she would go to lunch with him and then come back and have five or seven hundred dollars with her," said Conway. "He bought her a couple of cars – and helped her out pretty regularly for about five or six years."

Stahl's bank records indicated a withdrawal of $20,000 in cash from his checking account – an unusual transaction, considering his account history. According to his estate executor, that money was never located or associated with a corresponding expense. During the same time period, Vasco came to work wearing several pieces of brand-new jewellery.

Vasco even depended on Stahl to cover her living expenses, according to the manager of her Anaheim condominium building.

"She said, 'you don't have to worry about rent, he'll pay for my rent,'" said Burns. "I saw him, off and on, come to the apartment building. He tried to always sneak in and sneak out, because he didn't want people to see him. But then, later on in the relationship, I would see him at the pool with her and the kid."

Still, Vasco initially denied the affair when police questioned her about her relationship with Stahl. She claimed that she'd only spoken

to him on the morning before he was killed to discuss problems she
was having with a computer and printer he was helping her repair. She
added that Stahl had mentioned taking Oppy out for her birthday, but
insisted he hadn't told her where they would be going.

Only three months later, Vasco admitted to the affair. This time,
she told police that her relationship with Stahl ended in 1996, when
she claimed he refused to leave his wife. In another interview, in
October 2000, Vasco said that after she ended the affair with Stahl, she
began seeing another man named Greg Stewart.

Vasco and Stewart had met at a mental hospital. The relationship
between the two has been described as "tumultuous," plagued with
drug use and violence. During this relationship, court documents allege
that Vasco and Stahl remained close, and she said he "was always going
to be there" for her.

However, officers began to doubt Vasco's story after speaking with
her supervisor, Susana Torres-Bivian. According to Torres-Bivian,
Vasco claimed to still be "dating" Stahl in 1999 – detailing the
"long-term relationship" they had and giving Torres-Bivian the
impression that this affair was ongoing. Vasco had also asked
Torres-Bivian not to tell the police about her relationship with Stahl.

Torres-Bivian added that in the late summer of 1999, Vasco told
her she'd started dating "Tony," a maintenance worker in Vasco's
apartment building. It didn't conflict with her relationship with Stahl,
Torres-Bivian said Vasco claimed – the men knew each other and were
fine with the arrangement.

"Can you make her disappear?"

Vasco met Tony Satton when he used his maintenance man's
passkey to let himself into Vasco's Anaheim apartment to repair her
sink. When she told him not to barge into her home, "he responded by
going into her bedroom," said Fleeman in his book, *Deadly Mistress.*

"Well, it began that way, (and) every day after that he started
coming," Vasco recalled.

The relationship began innocently enough, with "civil" conversations whenever Satton dropped by. But eventually, he asked Vasco if she knew where he could buy marijuana. Since she'd started attending church and was living a sober life, Vasco told him she didn't – but she finally relented and sought out a dealer for Satton.

"That's how he started," she said. "And then he wanted some speed, so I got that for him, too... Before you know it, I started using again."

Vasco and Satton would get high together, and he would open up about his life back in North Carolina – past violence, encounters with police. He told her she needed to keep her mouth shut about his criminal history, even threatening to hurt Vasco's daughter, Ashley.

"He goes, 'I personally won't do it, but I'll have somebody come and get her and you'll never see her,'" said Vasco.

By this time, Stahl was getting desperate. His health was failing, and he wanted out of his stale marriage. Despite his healthy diet and daily exercise regimen, Stahl struggled with heart problems. At only 37 years old, Stahl underwent a triple-bypass surgery, followed by numerous angioplasty treatments. In July 1999, he pulled through a quadruple-bypass that doctors had given him only a 20 per cent chance of surviving.

"Stahl was going to die very soon," Villalobos said. "He wanted things to happen quickly."

Although legal records revealed that Stahl and Oppy had signed a prenuptial agreement, Stahl had told Vasco that he was afraid a divorce would "ruin him." He also admitted that his mother was very fond of Oppy, and she would be significantly hurt if he left his wife. That meant he needed to find another solution to free himself of his commitment to Oppy.

An electrician named Richard Anaya, who had previously been involved with a gang, told police that the doctor had made an "unusual late night proposal" after he'd been hired to do some electrical work about a year before the murders took place.

"He just said, 'I need somebody to take care of my wife, you know, she's making my life hell, and, you know, I was just wondering if you knew anybody,'" Anaya testified. "And I was like, 'wait a minute, man, are you joking around?'"

Anaya told the jury that he thought Stahl had been drinking, but that the look on Stahl's face was very serious. He led Stahl in a prayer and left – adding that he felt that Stahl's outlook had "improved."

In fact, Stahl was still determined to find a way out. Vasco recalled him saying, "that bitch, I can't stand her anymore. I want her gone. Can you make her disappear? Do you know anybody?"

At first, Vasco didn't. But as she learned more about Satton's violent past, it started to look as though there might be a solution to Stahl's problem. Satton claimed to have been part of an assassination group in North Carolina, and Vasco claimed she was drunk and on drugs when she told Satton about Stahl.

"He told me about people he had in Carolina that would take care of people," Vasco testified. "So I told him I have a doctor friend that wants to take care of his wife."

According to Vasco, she tried to back out of the arrangement by telling Satton that she was just kidding – but he refused to take no for an answer. She claimed he threatened to hurt her or her family if she didn't follow through, or if she told anyone about the deal. Eventually, Vasco said, Satton told her he needed money and demanded she get in touch with Stahl. Vasco complied.

"His demeanor, use of drugs, and paranoid behaviour alarmed her," said a court document, "and he routinely carried a shotgun at his side."

According to Detectives Villalobos and Meaney, the men allegedly came to an agreement – Stahl would pay Satton $30,000 to carry out the murder, then create a diversion and skip town.

Vasco told Stahl that Satton "was scary" and begged him to call off the plan. Instead, Stahl gave her an envelope full of cash and told her to deliver it to Satton. From then on, Vasco said, she didn't speak with either man about the arranged hit. In a statement to police, Vasco even claimed she was angry with Stahl for "putting her in the situation" which she felt was "wrong."

"I told (Stahl), 'please call it off,' and he wouldn't listen," she said. "I cried, 'please, please.' Nobody has any idea how bad I wanted to stop it."

In September, Vasco alleged, she successfully stalled a previous murder plot – and again attempted to persuade Stahl to back out of it again in November. This time, Stahl refused. According to Vasco's confession to police, Stahl pressured her by reminding her of everything he had done for her over their nine-year relationship.

"He just said, 'what about me? You want me to suffer all these years? You want to see me suffer the rest of my life?'" Vasco recalled, admitting that Stahl had been talking about killing his wife since as early as 1995.

However, Stahl was unaware that Vasco was having an affair with Satton – and Vasco didn't know that Satton was actually Dennis Earl Godley, a felon from Bellarthur, North Carolina, on the run from police in two states. She also didn't know about Godley's history of obsessive jealousy, when it came to his women.

Best laid plans

On November 19, Vasco had plans to visit with her daughter's grandmother, Nancy Stewart. The visit was cancelled, however, when Vasco told Nancy that she was feeling "stressed out" and needed some time to herself – to take a drive along the scenic Ortega Highway. According to an interview with the Orange County Register, she also met with Stahl and Godley to confirm the details of the planned hit.

According to Vasco's testimony, after meeting at the parking lot where Stahl and Godley first met, Stahl told her to drive up Ortega Highway while he followed close behind. When Godley told her to stop, he got out of the car and "took target practice at a sign." Vasco said she once again told Stahl about the threats Godley had made against her and her family, and begged him to reconsider.

The next day, Stahl called Vasco at work. Torres-Bivian said Vasco had left work early, so he said he would try her at home. According to Stahl's telephone records, he and Vasco spoke four or five times that day.

Vasco had plans that evening to attend a quinceanera with her neighbour, Belen Lopez. According to Lopez, Godley and Vasco stopped by the apartment to explain that they wouldn't be able to accompany her to the birthday party, claiming that they had "another commitment" to attend to. During this discussion, Lopez said, Godley was holding an empty shotgun case.

Godley and Vasco then went to a gas station on Ortega Highway, where they waited for the Stahls' car, a silver 1996 Dodge Stratus, to appear.

A big surprise

After celebrating Oppy's birthday at a restaurant in Mission Viejo, Stahl drove his wife east on Ortega Highway – a remote and winding road through the San Juan Capistrano foothills. They were headed away from their home, but Oppy didn't mind – she was glad to spend a romantic evening with her husband, whose history of infidelity had strained their marriage.

"She called that day and told us (Stahl) had a big surprise for her," said Linda Dubay, Oppy's sister. "She sounded hopeful."

The "big surprise" wouldn't be good for Oppy. Stahl pulled over onto the shoulder, leaving the engine running. Orange County sheriff's Captain Steve Carroll said that at this point, Stahl knew Vasco and Godley would show up to shoot his wife – "he's not expecting to get killed," Carroll added.

According to Vasco, she waited in the car while Godley approached the Stahls' car. She said she heard him ask if everything was okay, and then heard gunshots and Oppy's screams.

"She was saying, just, 'oh my god!' and yelling," Vasco said. "I didn't turn around. It was killing me."

Vasco claimed that she then contemplated leaving, but Godley returned to the car to reload his weapon – and pointed the gun at her. She said Godley asked her where she was going, and then said, "I was ready to pop you."

Godley then returned to Stahl's car, where Vasco heard him fire more gunshots. When he came back to the car, he told Vasco that he'd shot both Oppy and Stahl – to eliminate a potential witness. Detectives are still unsure if this is entirely true, or if Godley killed Stahl because he was jealous of the relationship between the doctor and Vasco.

"(Stahl) didn't see it coming," Villalobos said. "He thought he was taking care of her, and then – boom! – he got his."

According to Vasco, Godley had turned on Stahl because he hadn't followed the agreed-upon rules. During the hit, Godley had requested that Stahl keep his hands visible at all times by leaving them on the steering wheel – and when he didn't, Godley shot him.

Vasco gave Torres-Bivian a ride to work the Monday after the slayings, and according to Torres-Bivian, she appeared to be in shock as she told her about Stahl's death. Torres-Bivian said Vasco said "they" killed Stahl and his wife.

After committing the murders, Godley fled. Vasco told people that her relationship with "Tony" had ended after she'd caught him with another woman, but the two stayed in contact even after Godley returned to North Carolina.

The Weasel

Sergeant Ron Smith, with the Pitt County sheriff's department in Greenville, North Carolina, had been trying to arrest Godley for more than a year – ever since Godley had jumped through the window of his mobile home, kicked a deputy in the head, and disappeared into the surrounding woods.

"The Weasel – that's what we call him here, because he keeps escaping," Smith said. "In twenty years of service, he is one of the meanest men I have met. You look into his eyes, and they look black."

After Godley escaped, Smith asked informants across the county to tell him if the Weasel ever turned up again – and finally, in August 2000, Smith found him. The Weasel was finally brought in on robbery charges from nearly two years before, but it would be another two months before police would connect Godley to the murders in California.

An alert was sent from a department in Orange County, asking for help locating alleged murder suspect Tony Satton. The message was accompanied by a photograph of a man Smith had come to be very familiar with.

"Soon as I saw that picture, I knew it was the Weasel," Smith said.

Still, Godley denied his involvement with the murders during interviews with Meaney and Villalobos – but arrest warrants were issued for both Godley and Vasco on December 11.

"They are making it look like we (he and Vasco) were in this mad love affair and plotting and all these things," said Godley during a telephone interview from Tidewater Regional Jail in Suffolk, Virginia, where he awaited extradition following his arrest. "That's complete (baloney). I think it's a huge conspiracy and I'm the scapegoat."

Orange County police, however, were pleased to put the case behind them. According to Orange County Sheriff Michael Corona, "people who commit crimes like these need to know it may not be today, it may not be tomorrow – but someday, we are going to get them."

Learned helplessness

At her trial, Vasco testified that she didn't truly believe the murders would ever take place – and didn't intend the deaths of either victim. Her case was supported by a clinical psychologist, Dr. Nancy Kaser-Boyd, who specialized in family violence.

According to Kaser-Boyd, Vasco exhibited "common features" of both battered women's syndrome and post-traumatic stress disorder, including "learned helplessness" and denial. Kaser-Boyd claimed these stemmed from "repeated violent acts against her," including the abuse she suffered as a child as well as in a number of subsequent relationships.

Defense counsel used this to argue that Vasco "lacked the requisite intent" for a murder charge, and for the special circumstance allegations of lying in wait and multiple murder. The intimidation Vasco faced from Godley's persistent threats contributed to her "learned helplessness" and denial – demonstrating that she did not intend to help carry out the planned hit.

However, this defense was disputed by Deputy District Attorney Dennis Conway, who argued that Vasco was "not the type of woman where men can just march into your life and control you." He also informed the jury that Vasco had a past conviction of physically abusing a boyfriend.

The jury also heard from James Stewart, Vasco's daughter's paternal grandfather. In his testimony, he recalled going to a gun shop with Vasco in 1999. According to James, she'd pointed out a .357 Magnum revolver, claiming she'd bought the same kind of gun for her boyfriend, "Tony" – the same kind of gun that had been used to kill Stahl and Oppy.

"(Vasco) knew first-hand Godley was a dangerous, violent, paranoid sociopath," stated court documents. "The jury reasonably could conclude it was foreseeable such a violent individual would have an incentive to eliminate Stahl as a witness after Stahl paid him the entire amount under the murder contract."

A request was made by the defense to reduce Vasco's first-degree conviction for Oppy's murder, which would have made her eligible for parole after serving part of the sentences for each slaying. However,

Orange County Superior Court Judge Francisco P. Briseno denied the request.

According to a Los Angeles Times article published on November 26, 2002, Vasco "held her lawyer's hand and cried" as the jury read their verdict.

"She's a tough, street-smart person," said juror Donald Tobias, a retired chiropractor who lived in Placentia. "(The panel) felt that as long as she wasn't intoxicated or high, she had a pretty good idea this would happen."

Although Vasco's confession to police was thrown out by a judge who found that it had been "coerced," she was still convicted of first degree murder and was sentenced to life in prison with no possibility of parole. Godley pleaded guilty to murder, receiving the same sentence – however, he maintains that he only shot Stahl, claiming Oppy was murdered by Vasco.

"He recognized he committed this crime, and he's really remorseful for his part," said Godley's lawyer, Assistant Public Defender Denise Gragg.

KILLER BABE : THE TRUE STORY OF BRITTANY HOLBERG

96

Brittany Holberg was a twenty-three years old prostitute when she was convicted of murdering 80-year-old A.B. Towery Jr, stabbing him over sixty times.

The controversy surrounding the case centered around the relationship of Brittany and Towery prior to the killing. Brittany argued that Towery was a client who went into a rage when he found drugs on her person. He attacked her and she retaliated in self-defense.

Further investigation would reveal otherwise, however, as Brittany would use numerous household items in a brutal assault on the elderly man.

She fled the scene only to be caught at a McDonald's after police received a tip from a witness who saw her on "America's Most Wanted."

With her good looks and well-proportioned body, Brittany has remained in the spotlight as she was featured in a Maxim Magazine article as one of the "hottest women on death row".

Brittany still sits on death row today with her case being appealed on the numerous levels in the court system.

EARLY LIFE

Brittany was born on January 1, 1973, in Amarillo, Texas.

Accounts on Brittany's home life vary as she would manipulate according to the needs of her listener. To her probation officer, she informed them that her home life was "good" and that she "had everything that she ever wanted". She would often describe her mother as her best friend.

During other occasions, however, Brittany would paint a different story.

She would describe her parents as being "hippie-drugsters". Brittany would state that she was close to her mother but never knew her father, a heroin addict who was in and out of the Texas prison system. Her mother would later marry a man named John Schwartz with the couple marrying and divorcing four times.

They would drink heavily and openly smoke weed in front of the young Brittany who would be sexually assaulted by a babysitter at the age of five. When she was twelve, one of her aunts was murdered and according to Brittany "everything fell apart" at home. Her parents would leave her unattended as they indulged in pot and booze.

"They just stopped working," Brittany said. "They just let everything go."

She would be gang raped by two men who confronted her in an alley behind her home when she was thirteen.

Brittany would then spend the majority of her time living with her grandmother. By the age of sixteen, however, she would run away with her boyfriend Ward. The two would make it as far as California, get married, and have a young daughter named Mackenzie.

The union would not last long, however. Brittany would divorce Ward and move back to her native Amarillo. Ward would take Mackenzie and move to Tulsa, Oklahoma.

Brittany would state that she suffered a knee injury and would become addicted to pain medication during treatment. She would then graduate to harder drugs like cocaine.

In and out of rehab, Brittany's life spiraled out of control. She could manipulate with the best of them, however, and would escape from the Midland Halfway House with the help of a female counselor.

Brittany would hang out with the drug-using crowd and her own habits were out of control. To support her addiction, Brittany began working as a prostitute.

This would put her in harm's way on many an occasion as she would get gang-raped and beaten severely.

The assault would put her in the hospital but she would resume "tricking" when she was released.

"At that point in her life, Brittany was incorrigible," forensic psychologist Paula Orange said."Numerous people had reached to her and tried to help. She had extended family members trying to help. Friends trying to help. Even church outreach workers. All to no avail. The drugs had taken root and she was dead set on manipulating everyone around her. Family, roommates, church members, doctors, dentists, and pharmacists would all fall victim to her schemes to get drugs."

By 1993, Brittany was a full-blown drug-addicted prostitute with the rap sheet to prove it. In April of that year, she would steal a gun from her step-father. She then passed over $1300 in "hot" checks and applied for several store credit cards using a fake name.

Brittany and one of her aunts would run a scam on dentists, lying to them about their pain levels in order to get prescription medication. When the prescription drugs ran out, she would return to street drugs like cocaine and heroin. Arrests would follow and Brittany would be charged in Hale County with drug possession, paraphernalia, and public intoxication.

Upon her release, Brittany would proceed to steal her mother's car and forge checks in her name. The prostitution continued unabated as well as she stole the wallet from one of her "tricks" who pressed charges.

While in jail for the theft, Brittany would be introduced to Ella Gibbs and Patricia Karnes who ran the ministry in the Randall County Jail. The women tried to get Brittany on the right track and introduce her to Christianity.

"I wanted to reassure Brittany that she is a valuable person, that her life has great potential, and that this is the mortal portion of an eternal life," Karnes said. " Brittany is an eternal being and through the many prayers from my [prayer] group [in Lubbock,] I have been led to come back into this child's life to support her here, to encourage her, to find her courage from the Holy Spirit within her, and to let her know that there is a human being mortal person who will stand beside her and see the good in her and support whatever God plans for the rest of your [sic] life."

A.B. TOWERY

Towery was by all accounts a nice man. His son would bristle at the idea that he was Brittany's "sugar daddy".

"Dad wasn't a dirty old man," his son said. "Dad was just trying to help somebody and look what he got, and now she's getting three meals a day and a warm place to sleep."

The defense would later bring up the fact that he once pulled a knife on his son Russell during a temper tantrum. Towery would have a history with prostitutes (according to court testimony). Connie Baker would be a prostitute from the 1980s to 1997 and stated that Towery was one of her clients. Baker would also claim Tower as a client but she also had a history of drug possession and auto theft. Diana Wheeler would also admit to being one of Towery's prostitutes in the years of 1994 and 1995. She had come to his home and he even went so far as to clean the stains off his Mel Mac dinnerware. But Wheeler also had a long criminal history like Baker, arrested for prostitution, criminal trespass and giving false identification to a police officer.

The controversy at the trial was if Brittany and Towery had an ongoing "sex-for-money" relationship.

This would be vigorously discounted by family members.

His daughter-in-law would come to the home and help with some housekeeping. His sons would also visit daily and never report any "ladies of the evening" coming to visit their father.

The picture just didn't fit.

Brittany stated she was sent to Towery's place by a fellow streetwalker who went by the moniker of "Green Eyes" but that it was later revealed that no such prostitute by that name existed. Brittany had lied like she had so many times before.

The two seemed to have met by chance.

COMING BACK FROM THE GROCERY STORE

November 13th, 1996 was another normal day for the 80-year old A.B Towery. He had just purchased groceries at an Albertson's store and was walking back to his apartment. As he entered the courtyard, he was approached by the 23-year old Brittany Holberg.

She asked to use his telephone and Towery consented. He wanted to help the sweet-voiced Brittany and didn't believe that she posed any kind of physical threat to him.

What he didn't know was that Brittany was coming down from a cocaine high and had not slept in ten days.

"Brittany could be persuasive," Orange said. "She was well-versed in how to charm people, she knew exactly what to say and do in terms of body language. She was like a trained actress. It didn't take much cajoling on her part to convince Towery to let her inside his home. He probably thought 'what's the big deal?'"

Once inside, Brittany would demand money from the elderly man but he refused. Brittany then attacked Towery, trying to strong arm the wallet out of his pocket. The struggle began in the living room. The two then pushed and pulled each other around a partition that separated the kitchen from the living room. They then returned to the living room. At some point, Towery tried to leave the apartment but Brittany pulled him back in. The evidence also indicated that the two paused during this 45-minute fight, catching their breath and nursing their wounds. Brittany would sustain minor stab wounds to her stomach and thigh.

"This was most likely a fight that had a lot of clutching and grabbing," Orange said. "There was less blood in the living room so the conjecture is that is where the fight started. There was blood near the door so that suggests that Towery was bleeding out and trying to escape for help. Remember, he was a slow-moving 80-year old man. Brittany was a young woman but she was fueled by cocaine. He's getting tired a lot faster than she will."

Eventually, Brittany gained the upper hand. She used various objects around the home to beat down Towery. She started with a cast iron frying pan, then a steam iron, a claw hammer, a fruit knife, a butcher knife and then two forks. Towery would fall to the floor, a bloody mess.

Brittany then took a lamp and shoved its base five inches down his throat which choked him to death.

Satisfied that he had finally killed Tower, Brittany removed her bloody clothes. She washed up in his bathroom then went to his closet to find some clothes that fit her.

Walking back to his dead body, Brittany retrieved the wallet out of Towery's pocket. She took out the $1400 dollars he had and dropped the now empty wallet onto his stomach.

Brittany casually walked out of the apartment and hitched a ride with a young couple. The couple dropped her off at a local crack house where Brittany paid them off with two $100 bills (which had blood stains on them). Inside the drug den, Brittany befriended the proprietor and changed clothes again. She then went to a local hotel with hundreds of dollars worth of cocaine and indulged.

TRIAL

Brittany's defense attorney, Catherine Brown Dodson, would argue that Holberg acted in self-defense when she killed Towery. Her primary argument was that Towery was far from an innocent, elderly man. He was, in fact, a drug abuser himself who became physically violent with Brittany when he found a crack pipe on her person. He then hit Brittany two times in the head when she turned her back to him. Brittany retaliated and ultimately put the lamp post in his mouth in an attempt to end the fight.

Brittany then fled as she believed that no one would believe her side of the story because she was both a prostitute and a drug addict.

While in jail, Brittany would try to coerce Katina Dixon, her cellmate to kill Vickie Marie Kirkpatrick who was the prosecution witness.

Towery's history with prostitutes would be brought up in court testimony. They would also mention incidents of violence with his ex-wife and children but jurors didn't believe the old man was in any type of shape to employ the service of a prostitute.

"My father didn't even like the word 'sex'", one of his sons said. "He was old-fashioned."

A psychiatrist would testify, however, that Brittany had battered wife syndrome, post-traumatic stress disorder, and cocaine addiction.

The jury did not take long to deliberate, finding Brittany to be a cunning, manipulative liar who committed one of the most brutal crimes in the history of Amarillo.

They would find her guilty and Brittany would be moved to death row at Gatesville, Texas.

"I can't even explain to you," Brittany said in a magazine interview. "What it's like to have someone say 'You are sentenced to die.' It's words. You feel helpless, numb. It's almost as if your emotions shut you down."

Brittany would spend her first few weeks in prison laying prone on her bed in a zombie-like state. Over time, she grew accepting of her situation. She knew she was going to die but made it a point to learn to take each day one step at a time.

Her inspiration for cleaning up her act came from the memory of her daughter Mackenzie.

"I cannot live," Brittany said. "And I cannot die, knowing that my child has to live with the horror that these people tried to say about me, the story of the crime, their depiction that I was a cold-blooded person."

Brittany states that she dedicates her days to reading, writing to family and working on her law appeals. She also is anti-death penalty advocate.

She would follow other Texas inmates who were now on death row and make appeals on their behalf, specifically that of Betty Lou Beets.

"I realized," Brittany said. "It doesn't matter whether I'm guilty or innocent, this has now become a very political thing... At this point, they're just killing to kill."

She complained that after a recent jail uprising, the treatment of death row inmates has worsened.

"You would not believe the treatment we are given," Brittany said. "Just two weeks ago, we were informed that not only would we be strip-searched for our one hour of recreation a day, but also when taken for a shower. So for the last two weeks, we have been stripped no less than six times a day. This is every day, sometimes at times like 2:30-3 a.m., and we never leave the building or our cells for that matter."

As of this writing, Brittany's stay of execution has been appealed and appealed for the past eighteen years.

Her attorneys would exhaust the appeal process in the state system but it is now in the federal courts.

Her case, however, has been costing taxpayers "conservatively to be at least $400,000" according to county criminal attorney James Farren. In the future, he has decided to forgo seeking the death penalty in capital cases.

Farren continues to favor a death penalty but only under certain circumstances like "a guy walks into a day care center and kills the children or if someone kills a police officer or a firefighter in the line of duty."

Farren predicted that Brittany would remain on death row for another five years at least. "They can go through the U.S District Court in Amarillo, then it can go to the Fifth U.S Circuit Court and the U.S. Supreme Court. Then from there it can go back to the U.S. District."

But the appeals can come to a halt if the district judge refuses to hear it again.

"If the Supreme Court says 'no,'" Farren said. "That's when the district judge can feel safe in stopping this process."

The entire process has been an infuriating one for the Towery family. His son both rages and mourns about what happened to his father.

"She tried to apologize to us during the trial," Russel Towery said. " I got up and walked out. I'm sure other families are going through the same things I'm going through. It's been almost 19 years ... people forget."

"I don't want to die before she does. I want to stand there as she's kicking and screaming going to the death gurney. I want her to think about what my dad went through when she didn't even know his name," he said. "She thinks that because she said she was sorry, that everything's all right. ... she is evil and needs to be destroyed."

HUSBAND KILLER : THE TRUE STORY OF TRACEY GRISSOM

103

Claiming to be a victim of rape and other abuses, a distraught Tracey Grissom would travel to her ex-husband Hunter's workplace and shoot him six times in the back, receiving a twenty-five-year life sentence for his murder.

Her defense attorney would argue that Tracey was motivated by post-traumatic stress disorder caused by her Hunter's constant abuse and sexual assaults. One jury member had even asked the judge to be lenient in her sentencing as they were not allowed to hear details of her Hunter's alleged abuses (beatings, rape, sodomy).

But what really happened in the years that led up to May 15th, 2012? Was she in fact the victim of years of abuse by a psychotic husband? Or did she want to cash in on his $100,000 life insurance policy?

INSTANT ATTRACTION

The couple would meet during a dinner party in 2003 in Tuscaloosa, Alabama. Tracey was twenty-one years old and going through a divorce. She had a son, James Michael, from the previous marriage.

Family and friends would describe the union as "love at first sight." Hunter was blown away by the young Tracey's blue eyes and facial beauty.

"For him, it was love at first sight," crime author William Phelps said. "She was gorgeous."

A whirlwind courtship would ensue and the couple would elope in 2004.

"In the beginning, it was good," Tracey told CBS' 48 hours. "We had a friendship. Just your normal, honeymoon phase marriage."

"He was fun," Tracey said. "And he was attractive."

Hunter was two years younger than Tracey, however, and his mother felt that he had jumped the gun too early in the relationship.

Her words proved to be prophetic as after only eight months into the marriage, the marriage went south.

According to Tracey, their marital problems began with Hunter's drug addiction.

"I had caught him smoking marijuana," Tracey said. "Doing illegal things could cause a problem and I couldn't risk losing my son over."

Tracey claimed that she threatened her new spouse with a divorce but Hunter gave her his word that he would stop with his drug use. She stated that the relationship improved and the decided to start a construction company together.

"I took out an equity line to start a company," Tracey said. "Which was Grissom Construction. It was all in my name."

Hunter specialized in building elaborate boat docks. He had an artistic eye and could do docks, stairs, and other accouterments. The business began to grow in short order.

"They're going to take on the world," Phelps said. "They're going to be entrepreneurs and they're gonna make it."

They then had a daughter of their own, Anna Grace. The child was a long time coming for the couple. They had been trying for a long time as Tracey had five miscarriages before Anna Grace was born.

"She was premature," Tracey recalled. "Her heart and lungs were not developed. A very stressful time."

Behind closed doors things were rocky. On the surface, however, things looked good. They had a young family and were making money.

"All-American family," Phelps said. "White-picket fence. The whole nine yards. Middle-class. Suburbia. Maybe the Prince Charming that she's been waiting for."

But again, this was only on the surface. Tracey harbored secrets of her own. One of which was her own addiction to prescription drugs.

"Psychologically, there's something going on here," Phelps said. "There's something going on behind those beautiful eyes and it ain't good."

Tracey would often turn on on the children, showing off her temper. Then she would turn on Hunter.

"This would cause friction in the marriage," Phelps said. "And where there's friction, there's fire."

SETTING THE STAGE

Tracey would later state that Hunter would "act strangely" shortly before she filed divorce. She was a registered nurse and gave him an over-the-counter drug test. According to her, Hunter tested posted for marijuana, Oxycontin, opiates, and methamphetamine.

Hunter would later be arrested for marijuana possession but his family would insist that he never did the harder drugs.

Tracey would file for divorce in the summer of 2010 after six years of marriage. According to her, this would prompt physical abuse from Hunter.

Hunter had to move out but their divorce agreement would allow him access to the home.

"In September of 2010," Tracey recalled. "That was the first time he physically hit me. It (the abuse) got progressively worse. He had made the comments that if I told anybody he would kill me. I believed him."

Hunter' co-workers and family members would have a different take on the situation, however. His co-workers remembered a time when she tracked him down at one of the jobs and made a scene.

"She's screaming, jumping on him," Hunter's co-worker said. "Said something about him having another girlfriend and used the expression about, 'You are mine. I'll kill you. I'll kill you. You are mine."

"She's borderline demonic," Hunter's mother said. " mean, I absolutely believe—that she is that troubled."

Hunter's family continued to believe that he did not abuse Tracey.

"He did not have an abusive, an angry bone in his body," Hunter's aunt Gina said. "In fact, we kind of laughed at him because he was too laid-back."

The divorce was finalized in October of 2010.

EVIDENCE OF ABUSE?

Loran Richards was the first of Tracey's friends to notice the minor injuries on her body. She would inquire about the bruises but the answers she received were always evasive. Seeing Tracey with a black eye, however, forced her to try and get more answers.

"I said, Tracey, you may have terrible luck," Richards recalled. "But nobody is so unlucky that they trip, fall down the stairs, and hit their face on a baseball in the eye socket. So don't give me a lame excuse. You don't have to give me any excuse, but let's take a picture."

Tracey broke down. She gave her friend all of the grisly details, detailing the abuse she suffered at the hands of Hunter. Loran then became her advocate, taking pictures of Tracey's injuries. She would later state that she saw blood stains and other signs of abuse at Tracey's home.

THAT FATEFUL NIGHT

Now divorced, Hunter would arrive at Tracey's home on November 22nd, 2010.

According to Tracey, he then became enraged when Tracey told him that she had spent the night with a new lover.

"He told me that he was gonna kill me," Tracey recalled. Tracey stated that she tried to escape, running into the closet in order to "get away from the kids and to pray." Tracey's eleven-year-old son from a previous relationship was in the home as was the four-year-old daughter they have together.

Hunter caught up with her and knocked her to the ground. He tied a belt around her ankles and then began choking her.

Half-conscious, Tracey alleged to have been raped and sodomized.

The brutal attack would leave Tracey unconscious. She would wake up the next morning on the bathroom floor.

"I called Hunter," Tracey recalled. "I told him that I was bleeding and that I was hurt and that I needed help. And he told me, 'Fuck you. I hope you die."

Tracey wound up in the emergency room after the attack. Hospital records would show that she had a laceration on her head, bruises, and ligature marks on her feet.

Tracey would then be referred to the Turning Point domestic violence center.

Marian Waters would describe Tracey's injuries as among the worst she had ever seen in a twenty-year career.

Waters would testify that Tracey had suffered a horrific assault. She described her mental state as typical of someone who had just been raped; fearful, jumpy, fearing for her life.

Tracey had suffered a hematoma on her side that was the side of a grapefruit. She also claimed to have experienced rectal nerve damage which would require surgery as well as torn vaginal muscles requiring her to have a hysterectomy.

Police were called and Hunter would be arrested for rape, sodomy, kidnapping and domestic violence.

"And at that point, I feared for my life," Tracey recalled. "And I feared for my children's life."

A HIDDEN AGENDA

Hunter would be freed on bail but Tracey got a restraining order against him. She bought a gun and did not go anywhere unarmed.

She took photos of her injuries on the night of the alleged attack and texted them to Loran. Later, they would take more pictures.

Angered, Hunter would stop paying her spousal and child support. Tracey, however, may have had another scenario in mind for obtaining money.

She had forced Hunter to take out a $103,000 life insurance policy around the time their daughter was born.

On May 24, 2012, the day before Tracey shot Hunter, she would place a call to MetLife that was recorded.

"Thank you for calling MetLife, this is Pam. May I please have your name?"

"Tracey Grissom."

Tracey would then explain that she was angry that her husband stopped making payments on his policy. During their divorce proceedings, he had agreed to continue paying the premiums. Tracey stated she was calling to make sure that they had the correct address on file.

"Is there anything else I can do for you today?

"That's gonna be it!" Tracey said, hanging up.

"Well, May 14th was just like any other day," Tracey said, explaining the call to the insurance company. "However, I had moved four different times. Me and my children were running. We were running from Hunter. So I had called the company to let them know that they had my old address and to make an address change."

FALSE RAPE?

Shelly Standridge was hired by Hunter to defend him in the rape case. She would state that Hunter denied raping or even assaulting Tracey that night. Hunter did, however, admit to the fact that he and his wife had consensual sex that night...Rough consensual sex.

"So that night," Standridge said. "Hunter said that she was depressed and claiming she was going to kill herself. She was saying she wanted their relationship to work."

So she undressed in front of him. Her beauty was always impossible for Hunter to resist.

The two had sex despite Hunter having a new girlfriend at home.

Hunter's aunt, Gina, believed that Tracey wanted to kill Hunter before the rape case went to court.

"He had a new girlfriend, he was living with her," Phelps said. "He was moving on with his life. Hunter would claim that Tracey was jealous, obsessive, even stalked them."

"Hunter had moved on," Hunter's aunt said. "There was some court dates coming up that would prove that Hunter was innocent. There were court dates coming up that he would get visitation to his daughter. She had a lot to lose."

Tracey was on the anti-anxiety drug Klonopin. Hunter would tell his attorney that Tracey would take more than her prescribed dose. Because of this, she fell and cut her head. Hunter would then leave the house around 10:30 pm and go to his father's house. Tracey would call him hours later, at 3:20 am.

Hunter would state that Tracey had called to threaten him. She told him if he didn't want the responsibility of the children then she would make it where he would never be able to see them again.

Hunter's attorney did not know what Tracey's motive was for crying rape. She was very upset that he had a girlfriend.

MORE LIES...

Hunter would be arrested nearly twelve hours later, to his total shock.

Tracey would give her side of the story to the police which later is proven to be false.

She would tell police that Hunter had thrown her against the bathtub around 10 pm and claim to be unconscious until 4 am the next morning.

"But her phone records show she was on the phone all night, so she was never unconscious," Standridge said. "She was also using her data at 10:42 that night. She was using it again at 10:50 that night. ... She sends a text to her boyfriend at 1:49 am. She sends a text to her friend at 2:07 am. She sends another text to her boyfriend at 2:07 am."

Tracey would blame the calls on Hunter.

"All I do know is I was not the only person using my phone that night," Tracey said, suggesting that Hunter used her phone.

Medical records would show that Tracey's head wound was "purely superficial".

Only one suture was needed.

Furthermore, there was nothing on the medical record to support the fact that Tracey experienced vaginal and rectal tears. She did have bruises on her ankle and legs but the photos taken by police at the emergency room would not resemble the same photos that Tracey and her friend Loran would take days later. In the photos taken at the emergency room, an area of Tracey's body has no bruises. Days later, there is discoloration.

Tracey's attorney would blame the discrepancy on "blood thinners" which would cause Tracey to bruise easily.

There was also a discrepancy in her phone records. She would take a photo of her inner thigh, a deep bruise. This area of her body was not photographed by police during her emergency room visit. But on December 9th, almost two weeks later, Tracey took a photo of her inner thigh with the deep bruise

"He (Hunter) told me that he would make it to where nobody would ever want me," Tracey said after a 2010 attack. "I didn't report it because I thought he would kill me."

THE FINAL STRAW

Tracey woke up pissed on May 15th, 2012.

Hunter had been ordered to pay $2,100 a month for the rest of his life. He was not complying with the court order claiming that he was "out of work."

Tracey stated that she was on her way to a job interview when she saw a Grissom Construction sign out of the corner of her eye.

She stated that her initial plan was to take a photograph of Hunter at the job site in order to show proof that he was working as part of her litigation.

"I was getting ready to take the picture and when I looked up he was standing almost directly towards the front of the boat trailer," Tracey said. "He was looking back directly at me. He had this face, that's like mean - just, I don't know how to describe it. I mean, I see it over and over like it's right there all the time. He flipped me the bird, which to me was kinda like, 'Yeah I'm workin. Screw you.' And at that point, I panicked. At that point, I didn't know what else to do except to defend myself."

Tracey started firing. The first shot hit Hunter in the arm. He started to run and she fired again repeatedly. One of the bullets punctured Hunter's heart and he died of massive internal bleeding.

William Dockery was working with Hunter and was an eyewitness to the shooting. Hunter had turned to Dockery before the shooting and told him to "call the law". Before Dockery could pick up his cell phone, Tracey had commenced shooting.

Tracey then pulled out her own cell phone and called the cops on herself. She tearfully described that she had just murdered her husband.

CONFESSION

Tracey told detectives exactly what was going through her mind when she came upon Hunter at the construction site.

"Tell me about what happened," the detective said. "What led up to...what's going on."

"In November of 2010, he beat me unconscious and raped me...and, and left me for dead....and, and I finally pressed charges against him and he told me that he would make my life a living hell...and that's what he's done."

"What, what happened this morning that led up to you going..."

"I was going to work and I saw him...and he's been claiming that he-he's not working. And, so I pulled in there to take a picture of him...cause it was the truck that's still in my name...and the boat that's still in my name...and the trailer that's still in my name...He just stared at me and flipped me off...and I just went in there and shot him...I just shot him, I shot him, and I shot him."

Tracey would be distraught and tearful during her interrogation room confession. A few weeks later, however, she would call the insurance company to let them know that Hunter had died.

"Well, I was actually calling because I didn't know what I needed
to do ... Hunter passed away May 15th and I actually am going a court
case right now because it was due to self-defense..."

Hunter's family went ballistic over this. Tracey would claim that
she had no money but she continued to pay his life insurance
premiums.

"Even through the times when she's screamin' that she's destitute
and has no money ... she continued to pay life insurance premium,"
Hunter's mother said.

"I don't think my sister concocted a story," Tracey's sister said. "Just
so she could get insurance money. ... But that's all they (the
prosecution) had."

THE TRIAL

Tracey's allegations of rape and sodomy would not be allowed in
court testimony. She was allowed, however, to detail the effects of
Hunter's abuse on her were.

Taking the stand, Tracey would lift up her shirt in court and show
herself wearing a colostomy bag. She stated that she had undergone
several surgeries after her husband's daily rapes wherein she suffered
permanent rectal and vaginal damage.

Hunter's family was then allowed to speak at the hearing.

"This tremendous loss has changed me," Hunter's mother, Melanie
Garner said. "And I don't know how to change back."

Chloe, Hunter's sister, had a victim's services officer read her letter
in court.

"Tracey is psychotic," Chloe wrote. "She is the most selfish person
human being on this earth."

"Every mother should pray every night that your son doesn't fall
in love with someone like Tracey," Hunter's aunt, Gina Grissom said.
"There have been lots of allegations against Hunter. We've never
believed anything that has come out of her (Tracey's) mouth."

His aunt then looked directly at Tracey.

"Hunter was proud of his name. Why would you still choose to use our name, and bring it down?" suggesting that if Tracey hated him so much why didn't she go revert to her maiden name after the divorce.

The jurors would find Tracey guilty of murder. She would be sentenced to twenty-five years in prison.

One of the jurors, Janice Kelly, would contact Grissom's attorney Warren Freeman the morning after the trial. She had remorse over her decision and said that she wouldn't have convicted her had they had the rapes and abuse allegations been introduced as evidence.

"I feel I made a mistake," Kelly said. "If I had to do it over again, we'd have had a hung jury. We didn't get her side. She did not get a fair trial."

"We voted to convict because there was no dispute that Tracey shot Hunter," the jury foreman wrote in a letter that was addressed in the courthouse. "Jurors didn't believe prosecutor claims that she did it in order to collect a life insurance policy. We felt the shooting was a crime of passion, not for financial gain and that she should be sentenced accordingly. I wish we had seen evidence of the rape allegation. We feel that she just 'lost it.'"

"It's not fair, it's not fair!" Tracey sobbed as she was led out of the courthouse and to jail.

"We think the sentencing was too harsh," Tracey's attorney Warren Freeman said. "Considering you have the foreperson of the jury actually saying, we don't feel like she should be punished according to being found guilty of murder. Let's just say that there will be a basis for a new trial, and part of it will be something that the jurors saw that they weren't supposed to see and I'm going to just leave it at that until I file my motion."

"My son died running for his life," Hunter's mother said. "I don't know what was running through his mind but I hear him say 'momma.'"

"People who think that I murdered him in cold blood," Tracey said. "Either don't know the whole story or don't know everything that's happened.

Tracey was asked on CBS' 48 hours if she regretted pulling the trigger on that fateful day.

"No," she said flatly. "Because if I hadn't I would be dead. I truly believe that."

"She has a way of making everything she does look right," Hunter's aunt, Gina scoffed.

AMBER CUMMINGS

On the surface, James and Amber Cummings had it all.

They had been married for twelve years. James had inherited millions of dollars from his father and they owned a home in the peaceful, seaside town of Belfast, Maine.

"On paper, they were a couple that looked as if they had everything," forensic psychologist Paula Orange said. "Definitely one of those cases where looks are more than deceiving. They are downright deadly."

The couple met in Fort Bragg, California. Amber was a tall brunette while James was overweight and had an awkward vibe about him.

Amber found him charming, however, and would later describe him as the "nicest guy she'd ever met." She would marry him at 19 years of age and things looked bright for the young couple until Amber got pregnant.

"That is when his personality started to change," Orange said. "He would drive away Amber's family members in California and seek to keep her isolated. This brought much consternation to Amber's side of the family, obviously. There was one heart-breaking instance where Amber's mother and sister went to a neighbor's yard just to get a glimpse of Amber's daughter riding her tricycle."

James wanted no outside influence on Amber or their daughter so he began moving the family around. They left California when Amber turned five and moved to Texas. Then they traveled the country in a motor home until 2007 when the finally settled in Belfast, Maine.

"My husband said that he hated people and that he didn't care where we moved," Amber said. "I always wanted to live in a nice, small town in Maine."

EARLY LIFE

James' life seemed to have been one of trouble even though he was born into wealth.

His father would be murdered by one of his former employees in 1997 which was preceded by James making headline news as he videotaped his own mother doing heroin.

James would have numerous run-ins with the law himself.

"He had a bunch of assault charges," Orange said. "Some were cases where he was the victim. Others were cases where he was the perpetrator. When he was the perp, his father's money always bailed him out."

According to some Internet rumors, James' father had allegedly injured himself while getting off a forklift on one of the docks in the Fort Bragg harbor, breaking his knee in the fall.

Cummings then went to a friend's house and fell to the ground outside claiming that he "tripped in a hole." James' father then sued the owners of the property and won.

"That gives you an idea of the kind of guy James' father was," Orange said. "Rumors abound on the internet and in the Fort Bragg community about how he acquired his wealth. None of it is verifiable aside from the fact that the majority of the trust is funneled through a trailer park, which is odd."

Cummings Sr. would own many businesses and it would be one of his employees, a man named Williams Vargas who would gun him down.

Vargas detonated a homemade bomb he called a "firecracker" outside Cummings' home. The disgruntled employee then panicked as one of Cummings' neighbors drove by and blocked his escape. Cummings Sr. then came out with his own gun to investigate the blast which shattered his window.

Vargas then pulled out his own gun and shot Cummings. He had been working for Cummings at the Noyo Harbor trailer park and was allowed to live there in exchange for labor. But he began having problems with other residents which he would blame Cummings Sr. for.

Cummings, 77 years old at the time of his murder, had built his wealth by running restaurants, motels, a fish-processing plant as well as trailer parks. He also owned the Depot Mall shopping center and a McDonald's restaurant.

``Jim was quite an entrepreneur. He had quite a lot of land holdings, in some key areas, really, in the harbor and other areas around," former City Manager Gary Milliman said.

James Jr. would be the beneficiary of his father's death. He would tell people that he made his living "selling off Texas real estate" but the truth was that he was a trust fund kid living off the businesses that his father created.

The trust fund started off by giving Jams a whopping ten million dollars a year. The funds would deplete rapidly, however, as James would have a six-year legal battle against trustees whom he thought were mismanaging the money.

His mental illness would grow worse as his finances decreased.

NEO-NAZI SYMPATHIES

"He would go on daily rants about Barack Obama," Orange said. "Which would seem harmless at first until Amber realized that James was, in fact, a white supremacist. He began spending his days hunting down rare Nazi artifacts on the Internet and purchasing them."

James had applied to the National Socialist Movement, one of the largest neo-Nazi clubs in the country. He had written numerous white supremacy organizations on-line and began to mix toxic chemicals in their kitchen sink while telling Amber about his desire to make a "dirty bomb."

James had hired a pair of contractors to paint the interior of the house. The painters would later testify to witnessing James berate his wife. He would tell the men about his guns and go on about Adolf Hitler.

Thinking he had an eager audience, James bragged about his collection of silverware and plate settings that he claimed to have been used by Hitler himself.

"Check this out," James showed a swastika flag to the painter. "This was real. Not a knock-off. They actually waved this same flag while Hitler spoke."

James would run his household as if he were Hitler himself, marching around the home wearing a black hat and uniform with a Nazi armband.

Working himself up into a Nazi-like frenzy of rage, he would then abuse Amber physically, emotionally and sexually.

"He stripped away whatever self-esteem she had," Orange said. "He had no friends himself and didn't allow her to have any either."

As the years went by, James developed paranoid schizophrenic tendencies which had given birth to ideas that grew more bizarre with time. The married couple slept in separate bedrooms and James had guns placed under both of their pillows "just in case."

On one occasion, Amber left the home for an extended period of time. James immediately became enraged upon her arrival back. He demanded to know where she was and who she was with. Amber had gone to meet with a home-schooling group which they both previously agreed would be a good idea.

James went ballistic, berating Amber and throwing his sharpened Nazi knives against the wall.

CHILD ABUSE

James did not limit his abuse to Amber. His paranoid anger soon extended to their daughter, Clara.

This became evident to Amber when their daughter had come across James' collection of Nazi knives and began examining them.

"Leave those alone!" James screamed as he ran into the room and grabbed the box of knives away from the girl. "These belonged to the Führer! The Führer!"

Amber had very little self-esteem left, but she intervened when James would physically abuse their daughter. She would throw herself between the two and take the beating herself.

This would only incite James further as the would beat Amber then march up to Clara's room and continue his abuse.

"He kept them isolated and feeling helpless," Orange said. "They tried to escape on a few occasions but he caught them, keeping them locked in the house. She thought he had some kind of superhuman power."

CHILD PORNOGRAPHY

Seeking new outlets, James' mind became so perverted that he soon began indulging in child pornography. He showed his collection to Amber who shuddered in horror.

"Which one do you like best?" he would ask his wife, pointing to a series of pictures on the scream.

In addition to the child pornography, James began teaching his daughter to see the world through his racist viewpoint.

"This is equal-opportunity hatred," he preached to his daughter. "We can hate everybody."

"He was deluded," Orange said. "He actually saw himself as the second coming of Hitler. He began seeing his daughter as his future helper, someone who would be in charge of 'reconditioning' women and children after he declared war on the United States."

James wanted to build a torture chamber in the basement of the house. He told Amber about his desire to kill people and "peel the skin off their bones." He also obsessed on the Showtime television series, "Dexter", which featured a serial killer as the protagonist. James would then take long walks around the Belfast area, daydreaming about living out his 'Dexter' fantasy.

"He constantly talked about the different ways of killing and torturing people and hiding their bodies," Amber said. "He used to say it was a need in him."

THE FINAL STRAW

"The abuse happened incrementally for her," Orange said. "It is easy to sit back and judge a person like her, saying that she should have just left. But she was like a frog in a pot of cool water before it starts to boil. The abuse started small at first then bit by bit it increased as her self-esteem diminished. But when it came to protecting her daughter, she had to act."

One December 9th, 2008, Amber Cummings finally had enough.

She got up like she normally did after another night of abuse by her husband.

"Amber discovered James messing around with the chemicals in the kitchen," Orange said. "He said that he would bury her in the backyard if he said anything."

She sent her daughter downstairs to eat breakfast while she pulled out a .45 caliber pistol from underneath her pillow.

Then she held the gun underneath her own throat.

"Amber's first thought was to kill herself," Orange said. "But then she saw her daughter's doll in the room. She shuddered to think of her daughter spending the rest of her childhood with her father as she realized that it was only a matter of time before James' obsession with child pornography would make him do something to Clara. So she had to seek an alternative course of action."

Amber would later tell court-appointed psychologists that James' infatuation with child pornography and his "sexual attraction to young girls" made her believe that he was becoming obsessed with their daughter.

Fueled by her protective maternal instinct, Amber entered the bedroom where James was sleeping. She never had any gumption to stand up for herself when James abused her.

But when it came to protecting her daughter, a whole new Amber showed up.

She pointed the gun at the back of James' head and fired. Blood splattered against the bedpost. Shocked by her own display of violence, Amber sprinted down the steps and ordered her daughter to go to her neighbor's and stay there.

"If it wasn't for my daughter, I would have committed suicide years ago," Amber said. "Some of the mental torture will never leave me the rest of my life. It was so severe, it will be with me every day."

Amber then called the police and told them what she did.

"It's hard for us to justify shooting somebody who's asleep in the bed," Sheriff Jeffrey Trafton said. "But when we arrived she looked more like a victim than a killer."

"She was in a state of shock," Orange said. "She had finally taken action to free herself from years of abuse. The state, of course, cannot let such a deed go unchecked."

A CONSPIRACY AFOOT?

As police investigated the murder scene, they discovered another James Cummings secret.

He was gathering materials to make a "dirty bomb."

Fueled by his white supremacist ideology, James planned to go to Washington, D.C for Barack Obama's presidential inauguration. Once there, he would set off his dirty bomb.

"He had all the ingredients inside the garage," Orange said. "The FBI found the instructions for the dirty bomb. There were four 1-gallon containers with uranium, thorium and beryllium powder. There were numerous other jugs which contained lithium metal, thermite, magnesium ribbon, black iron oxide and other explosive substances. James Cummings meant business and there is clear evidence he was going to follow through on his plan. Whether he could have pulled it off is another story."

Had his plan gone to fruition, James could have potentially killed hundreds of people.

Amber saved not only herself but innumerable lives by killing James herself.

"The stuff that he had wasn't dangerous," Bangor Police Chief Jeffrey Trafton said. "In its present form, it wasn't dangerous to the community. Technicians told me what you had to do, you had to get real close for a long period of time before it would have any effect as far as the radioactivity. When the stuff was found, obviously detectives from the state police came and we didn't know what it was. But there was no danger to the community. That was established fairly quickly. But my involvement since it was handed over to the state police has been little to none."

THE TRIAL

Amber would remain in a state of shock after the murder. She worried more about her daughter's well-being than her own. She was fully prepared to go to jail.

"Her mental state was still askew after she killed James," Orange said. "She probably saw prison as a welcome respite from her abusive life. She had been in 'prison' already and saw the jail system as a safe place."

Amber would plead guilty during trial proceedings. Her story would make the media rounds, however, and she soon found numerous supporters in her small Maine town. People showed up wearing "Free Amber" t-shirts.

"There was no way in hell a jury in that vicinity would have found her guilty," Orange said. "None."

Amber seemed to have found leniency on both sides of the judicial system. Her attorney and the prosecutors would come up with a plea deal which called for a sentence of up to eight years but with Amber serving no less than a year. This would be followed by six years of probation.

Her attorney then recommended to the judge that Amber spend no whatsoever behind bars while the Assistant Attorney General, Leane Zania, wanted Cummings to spend a year in jail.

"This kind of 'self-help' is severely anti-social behavior," Zania wrote. "It will be punished accordingly."

During the course of the trial, Amber would not take the stand in her defense. Three mental health experts who had counseled her after the killing all affirmed the fact that Amber had endured traumatic abuse. They advised the judge not to send her to jail.

The psychiatrists had given Amber a diagnosis of "shared psychotic disorder" which in layman's terms meant that she had absorbed some of his craziness just by being around him.

"You don't hang out by the outhouse without getting a rash," Orange said. "So that is how Amber was able to endure all of that psychological trauma. She became so desensitized to it that it became the norm after a few years."

The judge sentenced her to eight years in prison but it was a suspended sentence, allowing her to go free.

"The terrible thing is, I was forced to take the life of someone that I loved very much to save my daughter that I love very much," Amber said. "It's something that I will have to live with for the rest of my life, and it won't be easy. I'll always wonder. I'll always be looking over my shoulder, always wondering if he can come back from the dead."

In her public remarks, Amber requested that the community forgive her husband and not have any anger toward him.

"I just want to thank the community and people of Maine," Amber said after leaving the courtroom. "Because without them, I don't think my daughter and I could have made all this progress. Really, really wonderful caring people. If I was anywhere else, we wouldn't be doing this well. I believe that with all my heart."

"The people around here are pretty incredible. They gave me the benefit of the doubt, and a chance to prove myself. There was a lot of support, an unbelievable amount of support, in Belfast. People came out and took care of us and made sure we had everything we need."

Amber stated that after she shot James that she fell into a "state of shock and numbness." She would continue to dream about James, having nightmares about him choking her.

Since then, she dedicated herself to trying to undo the mental damage James did to her daughter.

"I hope to raise a really good kid, who cares a lot about people," Amber said. I hope she ends up strong and can take care of herself. I think she will."

BONUS STORY: DEATH ROW GRANNY
It never ends.
No way.
No way am I letting this man demean and degrade me another day.
He's just like my father.
A binge drinker. And the binges were happening more and more.
He's on the road to nowhere and taking me with him.
It never ends.
First my father. Now him.
Fuck it.
I threw the cigarette on the blanket. I knew it was flammable.
Then I watched the smoke rise and smiled.

In Lumberton, North Carolina, Thomas Burke fell victim to a house fire which was caused by a burning cigarette. Investigative authorities thought that he had fallen asleep while smoking, leaving thirty-eight-year-old Velma Burke as his widow.

They didn't know that the fire was set by Velma.

Velma knew how to play the part of the grieving widow. She cried and gave the authorities the requisite crocodile tears. No one would believe that the murder of Thomas Burke would set off a series of killings performed by the seemingly kind and harmless church-going woman with the soft voice.

EARLY LIFE

Velma Bullard grew up as the second of nine children in the rural part of Sampson County, North Carolina.

Times were tough for the Bullard family. They would live on a small farm with no electricity, running water or an outhouse.

"They had to go outdoors," forensic psychologist Paula Orange said. "The entire family had to endure the indignity of going into the woods or using pots to shit and piss."

The home was small and cramped for the nine children. Velma would be forced to sleep in the same bedroom with her parents until the age of five.

Her father was a loom repairman (fixing an apparatus that was used to weave clothing) and an abusive alcoholic. Velma had an older brother, Olive, who were subject to his nightly beatings. Lillie, her mother, was too meek to protect her children from her husband's violent outbursts.

"She had the type of father who would not need any provocation," Orange said. "He would take out the pettiest frustrations, like not being able to find something around the house, and take it out on the children. Velma would become resentful toward her mother who was too weak or indifferent to stop her father from beating on the kids. She accepted his discipline as 'the way it was.'"

Velma would find school as a welcome escape from her dreadful home life. She loved her teacher and was an excellent student during her early grade school years. When she would return home from school, she took solace in the fact that her father would always arrive home late as he worked long hours at the textile mill.

"Her father Murphy had that Protestant work ethic in him," Orange said. "He accepted the long hours and low pay, seeing a kind of nobility in that. Only problem was, he would binge drink. Not store bought alcohol but homemade moonshine. After a couple of shots, he would be 'lit' and inflict his wrath on everyone in the house."

By the age of eleven, Velma would be forced to take on various chores around the farm. She would clean up the house, washing and iron everyone's clothing (eleven people). Her father would chastise her for not mending or sewing his work clothes properly as well.

"Her father was a stern taskmaster," Orange said. "Hell, you can say 'slave driver.' He would have Velma come home early from school days when the laundry got too backed up. Velma hated this and felt embarrassed. Her family didn't have much and as she grew older her classmates began to see her for what she was, a poor girl that was an easy mark for teasing."

Velma would grow to be 5'3" but gain weight as she got older. She would be mocked about her obesity, her shoddy clothes the gap between her two front teeth. She would also be called "knot head" after she ran head first into a boy at school which left a permanent contusion on her forehead.

By the age of twelve, Velma seemed to have taken on all of her mother's duties. She would cook all of the family meals in addition to performing cleaning around the farm house. She would miss school for days at a time as her father forced her to complete chores around the home before she could continue her education.

"Academic achievement was not at the forefront of her father's mind," Orange said. "Her mother was of little use because of her depression and mental illness. Velma was the oldest girl so she took on the duties of mom at an age where she should have been playing with dolls."

ANGER, ABUSE, AND CHURCH

Despite her father's verbal abuse and alcohol-fueled beatings, the family kept up a face of religious interest. Velma would be sent to Bible school every year until the age of thirteen. During her last year of Bible school, her father marked the occasion by buying Velma a silk pink dress with ribbons. Velma recalled the day as one of the happiest of her life.

The happiness would be short-lived.

Velma would claim that her father raped her when she was thirteen years old. She revealed this only to her pastor in her later years before she stood trial. Velma did not even tell her mother whom she did not think would believe the molestation took place.

"Things that went on inside our home when I grew up," Velma said. "Were kept inside."

At the age of fifteen, Velma continued to excel in school. Despite her chubby physique, she becomes adept at basketball and is pegged to be the team's star player for the upcoming season. But her father did not allow her to play.

"Who is going to iron these damn clothes?" he snarled.

The family then moved to Robeson county and switched from the Presbyterian denomination to Baptist. It was here that Velma would meet Thomas Burke and the two made it clear that they wanted to date. Once again, Velma's father would intervene, telling Velma that she had to wait until her sixteenth birthday until she could date.

The two waited patiently for her birthday to arrive and the following year Thomas would propose to her while they went to the movies.

Knowing that her father would not approve, Velma and Thomas eloped, moving to Dillon, South Carolina. Neither Thomas or Velma had any money as they both quit high school to get married. Thomas then went to work at a local textile mill.

"At this point, I believe that Velma began to realize that her life would not be that much better with Thomas," Orange said. "He literally has the same job as her father."

Economics forced Velma and Thomas to move in with his parents. This arrangement would last for a year until Thomas got a better paying job at a soft drink company.

At the age of nineteen, Velma would give birth to her first son, Ronnie. The couple would then move back to Parkton, North Carolina where they would remain in the same home for eleven years. Two years later, the young couple would welcome a daughter named Kim.

A CYCLE OF RELIGION AND ABUSE

The Burkes would be fixtures at the local Baptist church with Velma taking the reigns to teach a Sunday school class. But the prayers and sermons would do little to offset the growing ennui in the Burke home. Two years after giving birth to Kim, Velma would get hit by a drunk driver while crossing the street. She would be hospitalized for an extended period, suffering both physically and mentally.

Thomas' job at the soft drink company would not be enough to provide for the family. Velma would be forced to leave her small children at home and work in a textile mill just like her father. The couple would have different work hours, with Velma working nights and Thomas working days as they would take turns watching the children.

Velma would fall victim to the hard work at the mill and the stress of raising two young children. She began bleeding and her doctor performed a hysterectomy.

Velma's mother would take pity on the couple and give them one acre of land near their old farm. Thomas would build a three-bedroom home for the family but Velma was already going down a slippery slope. Her personality changed after the hysterectomy, claiming that she always felt "nervous and afraid."

Things would get worse as Thomas suffered a head injury in a car accident. He then began to drink heavily and begin to beat Velma.

"It was deja vu," Orange said. "Velma had, in essence, married her father."

One night, the couple argued and Thomas punched Velma in an alcohol-fueled tantrum. The police are called to the home and Velma sent Thomas to the state hospital to get treatment for his drinking. Her husband remains there for three days but when he returns home, his behavior is worse than behavior. He's angry at Velma for sending him to the "drunk tank". His alcoholism worsens and he would go on to lose his job because of absenteeism.

"Velma is thirty-five years old at this time," Orange said. "But she's an old thirty-five with crow's feet under her eyes and a hangdog look. She's had a rough life, not necessarily by her own design, and it has taken its toll."

Velma leaves the textile mill but then finds two different jobs in order to support the family. During the day, she works as a sales clerk in a Belk department store. At night, she goes to work as a machine operator in a cotton mill.

Thomas, meanwhile, would continue to drink.

He rages on a daily basis, on one occasion he pinned son Ronnie up against the wall and threatened him with a knife. Velma would faint during the encounter and be transported to the hospital. She was diagnosed as having a nervous breakdown and lapsed into a serious depression. The medical staff gave her tranquilizers to calm down. Velma believed that it was during this stint in the hospital that she became addicted to the painkillers.

"The drugs were helping," Orange said. "When nothing else did. So she wanted more and more."

Velma's children acknowledged that their mother's mood swings were due to the drugs.

Over the next three years, Velma would go in and out of the hospital for drug overdoses. After each visit, her addiction only grew as did her prescription list.

"She fell through the cracks in her own family," Orange said. "And in the system itself. Her family had their own issues to deal with as Thomas would abuse everyone on a daily basis. Finally, Velma did something she could control. She killed her husband."

On April 21st, 1969, Velma would drop a cigarette on the floor of her home and waited until her husband inhaled enough smoke to die.

His death, however, would do nothing to solve Velma's problems.

Her addictions and anxiety would only get worse.

A HOSPITAL FREQUENT FLYER

Velma would have another nervous breakdown after killing Thomas and lapse into a guilt-ridden depression. But seven months later, a co-worker at the Belk department store would introduce her to fifty-four-year-old Jennings Barfield. Jennings had emphysema and diabetes but Velma would marry him anyway. Unlike her marriage with Thomas which started out well, Velma's marriage with the older Jennings would be troubled from the start. Her drug addiction would escalate and Jennings would express his own regret at marrying her.

"I don't know why I married her," Jennings said. "All she does is pop pills all day."

After less than three years of marriage, Velma decided to part ways with Jennings. She didn't file for divorce, however, she decided to poison him with arsenic. She would later claim that she only meant to "make him sick."

Jennings Barfield was already ill and doctors had no suspicion that Velma was behind the death. Arsenic was a slow burn poison that could kill without detection. The autopsy called for no arsenic test and Velma had gotten away with murder once again.

But Seven months later, Velma would overdose on her prescription meds and become hospitalized. Her family recognized the pattern but could not wean Velma off of the drinks. She would remain hospitalized for three weeks.

Her personality seemed to change after the hospital release. She returned to work at Belk department store but kept being combative and argumentative with customers. Her boss knew of her circumstances and tried to coax her to do better. He took her away from the public contact and into the back stock room where he had her put pricing on the clothing items.

Her boss soon realized that Velma's addiction had gotten out of control. Velma would not be able to function in the back room, leaving tasks uncompleted as she would have her prescription medications delivered to the store.

"It is a hopeless situation," the store manager told Velma's son Ronnie before he fired his mother.

BROKE AND DESTITUTE

With no income, Velma would lose the family home as she no longer paid the mortgage. She would be forced to move back in with her parents and face the two people she blamed everything for.

Her father had grown ill, however, and would die from lung cancer shortly after Velma moved back into the home. She would feel bad about her father's death and admit that she had a love/hate relationship with him.

"I had learned to love him as much as I had hated him," Velma said. "He was so good to my kids. I think he tried to do with my kids like he wished he had done to us. He could not stand to see me correct them. If I would pick them up and spank them, he would ask me, 'Isn't that enough?'"

But after her father's death Velma self-medicated once again. She overdosed and was hospitalized for two weeks. Her family didn't judge, they instead thought she was "cursed."

"Velma needed psychiatric help," Orange said. "So she began medicating herself with deleterious results. She would "doctor shop" for different physicians who would be manipulated into giving her the drugs she wanted. Her addiction eventually grows until she becomes desperate for money in order to fuel the drug habit."

A MURDERER AND A THIEF

Velma began stealing from those closest to her, starting with her mother. Her mother confronted Velma about a missing check and Velma went ballistic.

"She had violent mood swings," Orange said. "The medication had completely changed her personality as she needed the drugs above all else. The people around her were not familiar with how to handle a person who had this kind of mental illness. So this made for a very dangerous cocktail for her and anyone close to her."

Hitting a new low, Velma took out a $1,000 loan under her mother Lillie's name. She put up the family home as collateral and forged her mother's signature on the documents. Velma then blew through the money and a month later took out another loan, once again using her mother's house as collateral. The following month, she emptied the checking account on her now deceased husband, Jennings. Two months later, the loan company began sending Velma overdue notices as she had not been paying off the loan.

"In Velma's mind," Orange said. "She had no other choice but to kill off her own mother."

Velma went to the local pharmacy and looked for bottles that had the warning of "fatal if ingested." She put the poison into a drink for her mother and watched as she drank the fatal elixir.

Her mother then began vomiting and lost control of her bowels. Within a few hours, her mother could not so much as walk and an ambulance was called.

Velma came to visit her in the hospital to finish the job. Armed with a Thermos, she made a special concoction of chicken soup and arsenic.

"Drink it slow," Velma said as she tenderly lifted the cups to the lips of her ailing mother. "Slow."

Her mother would eventually die of "natural causes" as no one suspected Velma of committing murder. Instead, she received sympathy.

"So sorry for your loss," hospital staff said.

"The thing with arsenic is that it shuts down the whole system," Orange said. "So hospital staff just chalked up her mother's weakness to old age. Checking for arsenic poisoning would be the furthest thing from their mind."

Velma showed the necessary emotion and received sympathy from friends and family. She then moved in with her daughter Kim and son-in-law Dennis who lived in a trailer park. She could not evade the authorities for long though as the authorities caught wind of Velma's check forgeries.

Velma reacted as she always did. She would run away and medicate herself.

"Her drug addiction kept pushing her into a corner and she saw no way out," Orange said. "So, this time, she goes to her son Ronnie's house and overdoses again, trying to kill herself. She falls and breaks her collar bone which laid her out in the hospital another three weeks."

But the police find her situation unsympathetic.

"We're sorry, Velma," the deputy informed her at her hospital bed. "But once you have been cleared for release, we will arrest you."

Velma would not have that. She tried to overdose again but this go around the hospital staff pumped out her stomach.

She was sent to court the next day and sentenced to six months in jail for the forgery. She is released after four months for good behavior.

NO REHAB HERE

Her addiction still unchecked, Velma returned to live with Kim and her son-in-law. She rummaged through the belongings of her son-in-law and stole a check, forging his name so she can get more prescription meds. Her daughter Kim now has caught wind of her mother's addiction, pleading with her doctors to stop prescribing her.

"In some ways," Orange said. "The doctors were just as guilty as she was. But back in the day, there was no way to cross-reference this stuff like we do now. Once she had her fill with one doctor she would go to the next and the next."

Velma's addiction prevented her from taking a forty-hour a week job. So she looked for alternative forms of income.

She would find a job taking care of the elderly.

Montgomery and Dolly Edwards would be her first clients.

"She found herself some easy targets," Orange said. "There didn't seem to be any legislative body in place that prevents sociopaths from caretaking the elderly. So Velma doesn't slip through any cracks, she just befriends the elderly couple and begins taking care of them."

Montgomery was blind and unable to walk. He was 93-years old and his 83-year old wife was too feeble to take care of him. They paid $75 a week for Velma to become their live-in caretaker.

All was good, at least in the beginning. But Dolly had a sharp tongue and would criticize Velma daily. Velma would keep a nice exterior unless confronted, saw Dolly has yet another wheel in her cycle of verbal abuse.

"It seemed to be a never-ending loop for her," Orange said. "Being forced to deal with verbally abusive people. Velma had long since snapped and Dollie simply had no idea who she was dealing with."

Velma began to plot out Montgomery and Dollie's demise until she meets their nephew, Stuart Taylor.

Stuart was already married but was blown away when he met the caretaker of his Aunt Dollie.

Velma would play it cool, stealing what she could from the couple in terms of petty cash and household items that had value. They outlived their usefulness to her within a year as Montgomery died of "natural causes". One month later, Dolly also passed away.

And again, no one suspected the sweet and soft-spoken Velma to have had anything to do with their deaths.

MOVING ON

Velma saw being a caretaker as a perfect front for her. She could steal as much money as she could and when the old folks detected something amiss she would simply poison them. After killing the Edwards' couple, she set the word out at church that she as available to be a caregiver. The pastor would refer her to Margie Lee Pittman who was seeking for a caregiver for her elderly parents, John Henry and Record Lee.

"She comes here twice a week," the pastor reassured Pittman. "She's a nice, kindly woman. You can't go wrong."

Pittman's father, John Henry Lee, was eighty years old when he discovered that his new caregiver had forged a $50 check on his account. He then fell violently ill, suffering through a spastic spell of vomiting, diarrhea, and convulsions. The doctors would chalk up his quick death to gastroenteritis but in fact, he had been poisoned with arsenic.

Velma played the caregiver role until his end. She attended his funeral and cried with the family, sending an ornate wreath (with money stolen from the dead man) to the proceedings.

For whatever reason, Velma spared Lee's wife and moved back to Lumberton, North Carolina to live in a trailer park. She began working as an aide in a nursing home and received word from Stuart that he was now a widow. The two began dating and she moved part of her belongings into his home.

"Stuart is a nice guy," Orange said. "He has no idea what kind of woman Velma is. She is so manipulative and cunning that the younger man is putty in her hands. So the relationship starts great as she reels him in with kindness and charm."

The couple are happy cohabitating until Stuart Stuart finds a letter addressed to Velma from the state penitentiary.

Curious, he began reading the correspondence and realized that is from a former cellmate of Velma.

Stuart became enraged. He threatened to "expose" Velma to all of his family and friends. Somehow, someway, however, she was able to calm him down.

He then found out that she had forged over $200 in checks on his account. The two argued but stayed together for the next two months.

"Velma had the Christian facade down pat," Orange said. "She asked Stuart to forgive her and the next thing you know they are going to a Rex Humbard revival. But before they went, she poured arsenic poison in both his beer and tea. She made sure he drank every drop."

Returning home from the revival, Stuart started to vomit on the drive home, the poison kicking in.

Velma had to keep the con going. She had to appear like a concerned girlfriend so she called up Stuart's daughter, Alice, later that night and told her that Stuart had came down with the flu.

Stuart's daughter expressed concern but Velma kept her at bay.

"Don't you worry now, honey. I'll take care of everything."

Stuart died the next day.

Velma would speak at Stuart's funeral and tearfully asked for his wedding band. His family graciously allowed her to have it and gave her $400 to help her cope with the grief.

But Alice knew her father was a picture of health. She vociferously argued for more tests beyond the standard autopsy and sure enough, arsenic had been found in Stuart's tissues.

On March 10th, 1978, the sheriffs arrived at Velma's home to bring her in for questioning. She was interrogated for over three hours, holding her ground. But she knows the evidence will trump her denials and tries to commit suicide after being released. This go around, however, her son Ronnie stopped her.

The sheriffs come to visit Velma again and she has one more surprise up her sleeve.

But Velma has one more surprise up her sleeve.

She would confess. Not only for the murder of Stuart but of six others.

"I set my first husband on fire," Velma confessed without an attorney present. "And I killed the rest of them."

"It was almost as if she wanted to be free of the guilt she had been carrying," Orange said. "Her confession seemed to take a burden off her back."

"The last ten years were like that," Velma said. "A drug nightmare. It was a case of not knowing where you are or what you've done."

The bodies of her victims were later exhumed and all tested positive for arsenic.

FACING THE GRIM REAPER

Velma's case would be prosecuted by Joe Freeman Britt, who was listed in the Guinness Book of World Records as the country's "deadliest prosecutor."

Velma would plead not guilty by reason of insanity but the court denied her plea.

"I needed to keep them sick until I could pay back the money I had stolen from them," Velma said. "I wanted to earn their thanks by nursing them back to health. I needed the money. I was addicted to pain killers. Anti-depressants. Amphetamines."

On November 23rd, 1978, Velma's trial would begin in Elizabethtown, North Carolina where she would be charged with the first-degree murder of her boyfriend, Stuart Taylor. The trial lasted seven days and the jury reached a verdict of guilty, placing her on death row at the age of 47. She was scheduled to be executed on February 3rd, 1979 but received a stay.

Velma would be sentenced to death and the verdict was appealed all the way to the U.S. Supreme court. Her attorney maintained that the jury had never been presented with the full extent of Velma's "addiction and background." Velma remained tight-lipped about that to everyone but her pastor. Her attorney felt thought her horrific background could have been used as part of her defense and the jury would have found her to be more of a sympathetic case.

CHANGING SPOTS?

"She's not the same person who went to prison in 1978," Kim Burke Norton, Velma's daughter said.

While in jail, Velma became a model prisoner.

"The first week I was here was the worst week," Velma recalled. "Everything about it."

Velma no longer had access to her drugs in prison and she began to dry out. With daily visits from two different pastors, Velma began to discuss her anger and repressed issues that fueled her addiction and murders.

Velma would claim that as she was awaiting trial in 1978 she came to a "meeting with Christ" that caused her to "change inwardly."

Velma heard a broadcast by radio evangelist JK Kinkle. "Jesus loves you, prisoners, too," Kinkle said. "He died for you too. No matter what you've done, the Lord will forgive you."

After Velma heard this sermon, she dropped to her knees and cried out to God.

She would then become the "go to" counselor for young inmates in the prison.

The inmates would nickname Velma as "Mama Margie" because of her wisdom and she would in turn think of them as her "adopted children."

The prison guards and counselors would take the most incorrigible prisoners and place them in a cell next to Velma. Velma would invariably counsel the young prisoner and advise them on the correct path.

"They'd come in ready to kill themselves," Sister Mary Teresa Floyd said. "And here she was with a death sentence, mothering and helping them."

"Living in prison is a struggle," Velma said. "Even at its best. And I know that without Him and His strength that has sustained me, I couldn't have made it even this far."

Her stay on death row soon became a part of the news brief. During this time, a phalanx of evangelists would take her cause to the mainstream. The Reverend Hugh Hoyle would become Velma's personal minister as she received stays of execution in September, October and December of 1981. She would also have a letter correspondence with Ruth Graham, Billy Graham's wife as well as meeting their daughter Ann.

While Velma impressed the Christian do-gooders, the family members of the victims were not taken in by her "conversion."

"She's got religion now, they say," Margie Lee Pittman said. "Well, she had religion before. So we all thought."

A few more stays were granted until 1984 when the U.S. Supreme Court justice Warren Burger granted her a stay until August of that year. At this point, however, her execution seemed inevitable. In an ironic move, Velma would choose poison rather than the gas chamber and enjoyed the final visits from her children and grandchildren.

During the final week before her execution, the Reverend Hoyle, and his wife came to the prison with a battery-powered portable keyboard. His wife played the little organ then the Reverend sang "He Hideth My Soul" and "He is So precious to Me" in the cramped visitor booth.

Velma sang along, whistling in the graveyard before the reaper came for her.

She then wrote letters to each of the victim's family asking them for forgiveness. Reverend Hoyle would deliver the letters to the families, all of whom would refuse them.

MEET THE HANGMAN

As her execution date neared, Velma was placed in a solitary cell that stood directly across from the death chamber.

"It's total isolation," Velma said. "From everyone I had been with for six years."

North Carolina Governor James B.Hunt would reject her final plea for clemency.

On the day of her execution, the jail house would turn into a media frenzy. Death penalty advocates gathered outside the prison and chanted "Hip, hip, hurrah...K-I-L-L" while some sloganeered with "burn, bitch, burn". The protesters held up a few placards that quote Romans ch.13 which ironically was a verse that Velma would repeat to guards during her prison stay.

"For rulers are not a terror to good works, but to the evil…(The ruler) beareth no the sword in vain, for he is the minister of God, a revenger to execute wrath upon him that doeth evil."

The execution was scheduled to take place at 2:00 a.m but the protesters remained outside, their chants reduced to a simple "Kill her! Kill her!"

On November 2nd, 1984, Velma would be executed by lethal injection. The prison official came out and addressed the press, giving out copies of Barfield's statement of apology. The reporters then eagerly anticipated what Velma requested for her last meal. Initially, Velma just wanted the normally scheduled prison food; chicken livers, collard greens and a sheet cake with peanut butter icing. The last meal was delivered but Velma immediately lost her appetite. Instead, she opted for Cheese Doodles and a glass of Coca-Cola.

"Her attorney believed that Velma could have done some good in life," Orange said. "He stated that she could have become a teacher, counselor or a pastor. But her father set her on a path of self-destruction that she couldn't escape from. By the time she the left that road to ruin, she was too far gone in terms of her murderous acts. Justice had to be served in the end. In the end, the law doesn't care how genuine you are in your pleas for forgiveness. It only cares about the rule of law."

"I'm sorry for the hurt that I've caused," Velma said before her execution. "So many people, today if it were possible, I wish I could take every bit of hurt on myself."

GOD TOLD ME TO: THE TRUE STORY OF GWEN HENDRICKS

140

Gwen Gillespie Hendricks was born into a Navy family in Memphis, Tennessee in 1955.

Her father was a naval officer while her mother was a housewife. Like most military families, they moved often from station to station, according to her father's assignment. Growing up in a devoutly Catholic home and Gwen would embrace the religion with fervor.

Gwen dressed with modesty, wearing button down shirts and minimal make-up. She fostered a nerd look, with wire-rimmed glasses and short hair.

Carrying on the family's military tradition, she joined the Air Force at the age of twenty-five. It was there she would meet Jim Hendricks, twenty-four, who was her instructor.

Jim Hendricks was a tall, strapping Air Force sergeant with an air of authority. He had an easy smile and Gwen found him easy on the eyes.

"Well, it was kind of instant attraction," Gwen recalled. "There was a bit of lust there as he's a very tall, handsome man. The Air Force can tell you that you can't date but they can't tell you who to marry so I went to the Jag office and asked if I could marry my STA and they said 'yes.'"

The two were married in 1980. Jim had a five year old daughter, Season Hendricks, from a previous relationship. In 1982, they would have a son, Ben.

Because of their career choice, the couple spent a lot of time apart during the early years of their marriage. Jim was stationed at Wake Island while Gwen was assigned to Eglin Air Force Base in Florida.

The couple would be reunited in 1986 as Jim was assigned to the Air Force Academy in Colorado Springs. Gwen would not re-enlist in the Air Force, instead taking a job with the Internal Revenue Service.

The couple spent three years in Colorado before Jim would be transferred to Guam in August of 1989. He took the the entire family with him to the island.

"I figured we had a pretty normal family," Season said. "Until we moved to Guam. Things started to change. She (Gwen) would pick fights. She was jealous of the time my Dad and I would spend together."

"She (Gwen) had a different life in mind for herself," forensic psychologist Joyce Smith said. "She was used to having her own money. So when they moved to Guam there was little to do and less money to do it with."

Gwen and the children moved back to the United States, returning to Colorado and leaving Jim in Guam.

She would buy a home in Littleton and once again start working for the IRS. She then joined the junior Chamber of Commerce where she met Terry Knaack and a woman named Rochelle.

"Rochelle was into tarot cards," Gwen said. "And Terry was into new age occultism. My religion, my faith was still very meaningful to me. I wanted to do Bible study with them to get them out of what I considered witchcraft. Rochelle said she wouldn't go to Bible study with me unless I did the cards with her and the same with Terry. So I think I opened up the door to hell. Right after I started, everything went wrong"

During this time, Gwen began to experience health issues. She suffered from dizzy spells and nausea.

Her personality shifted as well, changing from being even-tempered to easily agitated and manic. With her health and ability to focus effected, Gwen stepped down from her revenue collector position to tax examiner.

"Could the illness have played a part in her deciding to kill her husband?" Smith asked. "Maybe. But Gwen was really steeped into religion and sounded like she embraced some of the more fringe elements of Christianity. She truly believed that occultism was a form of witchcraft and that those things could do her harm. So when she suffered from her illness she erroneously attributed it to her dabbling in the occult. She was a woman who preferred supernatural explanations to rational thought."

Gwen also started to grow deeper into debt, buying expensive gifts for friends.

In the fall of 1990, Gwen hired Terry Knaack to help remodel the Littleton home. A few months later, Knaack moved into the couple's basement with the rationale being he would be able to help with the mortgage. With the husband away and a man in the home, Gwen began to fantasize about Terry and starting over with him.

"Terry would talk a lot about wanting to having a ranch for children with special needs," Gwen recalled. "And I started having delusions that he and I would start this ranch together for the children."

"She entered into a fantasy world," Smith said. "She began imagining a life with this other man, having delusions of grandeur of what they would do together. He became her willing accomplice in her dreams, since her own husband was absent because of military duty. So an alternate universe with Terry Knaack became her obsession. What probably started as harmless day dreams soon grew into something sinister."

"I also believe that Gwen had more than a little bit of a Messiah complex. She had this compulsion to save people and it manifested in doling out gifts and handouts to people who she felt were in need. She had this secret life and kept things from Jim who was away on military assignment. Those secrets involved getting into credit card debt."

By January of 1991, Gwen began telling friends that she was having premonitions of Jim dying in a plane crash.

"I had this really bad dream over and over again," Gwen recalled. "Where Jim had died in a plane crash. I was thinking, well after Jim died that I would marry Terry and we'd start this ranch but of course Terry didn't know anything about because it was all in my head."

Gwen then began hearing voices.

"They (the voices) wanted me to sacrifice what was most dear in my life," Gwen recalled. "I remember thinking that I have to answer these voices because this is coming from God. You know, I've got to sacrifice what I loved the most and that was Jim."

Gwen kept a journal where she logged the "premonitions" of her husband's death. She titled the journal "The Courage to Will and Persevere," She described the voices that she heard and believed that God had told her to kill Jim.

"She experienced what we call 'command hallucinations,'" said Smith. "These are sometimes coupled with someone's value system, in this case, it was Gwen's religion. Gwen believed that she should obey God and believed that the voices that she heard were, in fact, coming from God. So this could go bad real quick if those voices told her to do damage to someone."

"She was past the breaking point, a delusional schizophrenic that was not diagnosed. When she confided with friends it was probably with people who shared her same point of view, people who believed in visions, messages from God and premonitions. Gwen was a soft-spoken woman and even if someone thought she was crazy they would not think she would be capable of taking a gun and blowing someone's brains out. She didn't have that violent vibe."

But behind closed doors, Gwen would deal with problems or difficulties in a haphazard fashion. She would often open up the Bible and believed that whatever random verse she came upon was a direct message from God.

"I reread Psalm 90 quite a few times before a small voice said, 'Keep reading, keep reading.'" Gwen wrote in her journal. "After reading the first page of stanzas, I knew I would be protected from the car bombs, the knifings, the guns, the contracts and all the other evil I had seen connected with busting the pornographers and pimps. Those mafia guys play rough, but somehow they just won't be able to get me. Then I turned the page to continue reading. It felt like a giant fist had slammed into my heart. I literally could not breath [sic]. I burst into sobs and sunk to the floor. I cried for Jim because he really was going to die."

Gwen began to prepare for Jim's death, taking out a $300,000 life insurance policy on her husband payable on his death.

She then visited a local banker, informing him that she would be soon be receiving proceeds from insurance claim. Gwen was told that she would not be able to use the money as long as Jim was alive. She then forged a doctor's note which alleged that she had multiple sclerosis. She submitted this note to the Red Cross along with a letter stating that they should be responsible for being her husband back from Guam.

Gwen did not want the proceeds from the insurance for her own material gain. She believed that she could use the proceeds from his life insurance to establish the "James Hendricks Foundation" to aid victims of mafia produced pornography.

"She became obsessed with pornographers," Smith said. "Like most people with Messiah Complexes, she chose an ill of society and focused on that, believing that she was a chosen vessel to help eradicate the 'sin'. In her deluded mind, she needed this money to accommodate

God's will to establish this ranch wherein she would save victims of pornography. The only way she could attain this goal would be to kill Jim and take the life insurance proceeds."

"I was very desperate to have him (Jim) back," Gwen said. "I felt like I was at my limit and not really realizing that I actually was really having a breakdown."

With her husband not even dead yet, Gwen began purchasing clothes for herself and the children to wear for his funeral.

She bought silk flowers and boxes of Kleenex for mourning friends and family.

Gwen also increased the amount of Jim's life insurance from $300,000 to $1,000,000.

True to her premonition, she bought a wedding dress for herself and put a wedding ring on layaway for Knaack.

Gwen would ask God to speak to her directly and "guide her hand" as she thumbed through her Bible. When she got to a passage, she would believe that was what God wanted her to study."

"For the first reading, only the last sentence made sense," Gwen wrote. "I had asked if what I felt about Jim's death was real. He said yes.

God can even speak through the dictionary!

After reading the first page of stanzas, I knew I would be protected from car bombs, the knifings, the guns, the contracts and all the other evil I had seen connected with busting pornographers and pimps. Those Mafia guys play rough, but somehow they just won't be able to get me."

"You can see her delusions of grandeur in her journal writings," Smith said. "She had all of the symptoms of a delusional narcissist, truly believing that God made her as the 'Chosen One.'"

Gwen would write that she had a two-way conversation with God about creating the ranch.

*"Oh, so the ranch is in Douglas county near to the Springs so my
family will be protected from the mafia guys' Then I knew in Denver, I'm
Gwen Hendricks. In the Springs, I'm Gwen Knaack. I had thought the
clinic would carry the name of the ranch, but with this new insight, I knew
that for safety sake, everything had to be kept separate."*

She continued to have health issues as well, as the nausea and
attacks of dizziness still had not subsided. Physicians could not
determine the cause of her illness. She was eventually diagnosed with
Ménière's disease, an ailment that causes vertigo and a fluctuating
hearing loss. She had a micro-shunt placed into her ear which only
helped relieve the pain she was experiencing.

Her mental health, however, continued to deteriorate.

Jim would return to Colorado for good in May of 1991. It would
not be a well-received reunion, however, as the couple fought over
everything specifically the living arrangements of Knaack. Jim
promptly kicked the boarder out of the home.

He then took control of the finances as he discovered that Gwen
had maxed out the credit cards.

"My brother said that she had apparently taken several other credit
cards and had maxed them out to the limit," recalled Steve Hendricks,
Jim's brother. "And he was furious with her at that point. He did
confide in me that he was thinking about leaving Gwen."

Jim would take away all of Gwen's credit cards and this made her
extremely angry.

"He took away her power," Smith said. "She got an ego boost by
buying expensive gifts for friends and helping out women that she
thought were in need. When Jim took that away, she saw him as
someone who needed to be eliminated."

Divorce seemed imminent but Gwen seemed immune to it all in
her journal writings.

"The funeral, the ranch school, children, the foundation, always being pushed forward," she wrote. "I have to do what I have to do, too. But just for now I'm going to take one day at a time. I'm hoping I don't get too compulsed to do anything more for at least this coming week. I need to rest.

Perhaps I should start by explaining the little voice. It's my voice, but not me. It comes from somewhere inside, and if I don't listen to it, act on it, it becomes a compulsion. If I don't listen and act on the compulsion, it grows stronger and stronger until it dominates all aspects of my life. I learned long ago to listen and do what I'm told. Things work out when I do, and when I don't, things get real miserable...Yes, my little voice is the way God reaches me with the Holy Spirit."

With Jim now home on a permanent basis, The voices in her head grew louder. They began to speak with more urgency in telling her that she had to kill her husband.

"True to her religious background, she did not interpret auditory hallucinations as a sign of mental illness," Smith said. "Gwen was the kind of woman who took the stories in the Bible literally, seeing herself as a modern day Abraham who heard voices from God. You hear it in the way she describes the voices in her head telling her to sacrifice her husband in the same way the Bible speaks of God telling Abraham to sacrifice his son Isaac."

"I said 'Lord I surrender to you,'" Gwen recalled. "I'm hearing voices from God and this is what God wants and I have to get this from God and if this is what God wants then I have to give it to him. So I went out and I bought a gun"

"The voices in her head told her it was time," Smith said. "And true to her value system, she had to obey. For her religion was not a therapeutic aid because of the way she had viewed it. Her God was a vengeful one, a violent one."

On Friday, August 17th, 1991 Gwen drove to Peterson Air Force Base to meet with her husband, a 75 mile drive, to bring him a change of clothes.

"Jim was working late and he asked me to bring him something to eat." Gwen said.

She had informed police that Jim was working all night to prepare for an inspection but changed his mind.

Gwen wrote in her journal about the incident.

When Jim called to say he was on his way home, I went into shock. I knew the time was at hand. I knew I wasn't really ready. I screamed and cried and raged. Then I asked again, if he was meant to die or was I just suckered into some kind of head game. Benjamin's daddy died. I cried myself to sleep that night. I thought what was I supposed to do with two husbands. God has the oddest sense of humor."

"She told me that she was gonna make a nice little picnic for them," Gwen's step-daughter Season recalled. "They were going to make a night of it and that she wanted him to feel good for his inspection."

Gwen left the home and dropped off both Season and son Ben with a friend. When Gwen arrived at the Air Force base, however, she stated that Jim told her that he was heading home. She maintained that the two then went back home in separate cars.

"His truck was in the lead," Gwen said. "I was in the car behind. I remember being so tired, I told him I can't go on anymore. I just want a quick nap and let's get in the back of the truck."

She said that they traveled in separate cars but she became tired and slept through the night at a rest stop along Interstate 25.

Police, however, believed that Gwen lured Jim to an abandoned stretch of highway with the promise of sex.

The two met at the side of the road and Gwen hesitated when thinking of pulling out the gun. She wanted her husband to go peacefully.

"I took the gun out from underneath the seat of the car," Gwen said. "I got into the truck and laid next to him and when I could feel that he was deeply sleeping that's when I shot him."

Gwen would shoot Jim six times.

"It was like I was outside of myself," Gwen said. "Looking and watching what I was doing. I felt very numb, very cold, like I was on auto-pilot. I got back into my car and I took apart the gun and I was just throwing the parts out the window and just driving around, just in a fog, not knowing what I was doing, where I was going. I stopped at a roadside rest stop. Fell asleep. When I woke up and I didn't know everything that happened."

When Gwen arrived back home that Saturday she began making calls to the police, stating that her husband was missing.

On Monday morning, she called Jim's supervisor who sent out two officers to search for him.

One of his co-workers would find his pickup truck on the side of Highway 83 in Douglas County. His body had been placed in the camper shell in back of his truck.

He had been shot six times in the chest and neck with a small caliber handgun.

Gwen would become the primary suspect.

Police noted that she hardly showed any emotion when they informed her of her husband's death.

"Her state of mind was that of a wife with a missing husband," one of the deputies recalled. "When she was telling a story, she couldn't stick with the same story. And that's a clue, obviously, to law enforcement."

Gwen would then break the news to Jim's daughter, Season.

"Gwen said they found him by the side of the road in his car," Season said. "And that he had been murdered. I don't remember her crying. It was the worst moment of my life."

Terry Knaack would be helpful in the case against Gwen. She had been secretly in love with him and given him her diary. He read through her writings and promptly delivered the diary to the Douglas County Sheriff's Department. The sheriffs then instructed him to call Gwen while they would listen in.

Gwen would tell Knaack that she didn't kill Jim but that she wanted to die. Then Douglas County Sheriff's Department Kim Castellano's intuition told her something was wrong. The Hendricks had two pre-teens, a boy and a girl and the boy was never around during questioning.

Castellano believed that Gwen had a problem with males. With one of the male investigators, an Air Force official, by her side, Castellano went back to talk to Gwen.

Once again, the boy was not there. Gwen was overly polite to Castellano, asking her if she wanted anything to eat and jumping up to fix her something before she could answer.

Gwen would totally ignored the male detective.

Castellano used this knowledge to her advantage and befriended Gwen, sensing that the delusional woman would be much more forthcoming with a female officer than a male.

Gwen began trusting her enough that she asked for Castellano's help in balancing her check book. The detective then saw that Hendricks had recently taken out several insurance policies that would be hers when her husband died.

The investigators then used a technique police refer to as the "midnight confession." Castellano and the Air Force official went over to the Hendricks house at eleven at night, waking Gwen up.

Questioning her in the family room, Gwen continued to deny her involvement in her husband's killing. Castellano and her partner then took turns reading from Gwen's journal, tightening the screws on her denial. They also saw Jim's watch on the counter.

Castellano then told her to get dressed and that she was being taken in.

Gwen finally cracked. She curled into a fetal position and confessed.

"Two stories that night—the story of the rest area and the story of Highway 83," she sobbed.

Gwen would go on to describe the highway story.

"There is blood everywhere, I can see it everywhere," she said. "It's terrible. My mind won't let me remember. I don't know if I shot him or not. I don't know what's real anymore."

Gwen was then taken to a local hospital where she stayed for two days for a mental health evaluation. She was arrested upon release and charged with her husband's murder.

After undergoing another mental health examination, Gwen was deemed delusional but understood the charges being levied against her.

Because of this, she was found fit to stand trial.

In court, however, Gwen continued to state that she didn't kill her husband. She said that the body found at the crime scene was not Jim's.

"There was the obvious choice for her attorneys to declare her insane," Smith said. "She had one hell of an imagination and could make things up on the fly. She said during the trial that she became completely convinced that her husband was still alive, going into full blown denial. 'He's still alive, he's out there somewhere and you have to find him', she would say. She was completely delusional."

Her first attorney, Lloyd Boyer, stated that it was physically impossible for Gwen to have murdered Jim Hendricks.

"The lack of gunshot residue inside the Capitol (Jim's car) vehicle," Boyer said. "Indicated that the murder had not occurred in the vehicle. Mr. Hendricks was quite a bit larger than Gwen and she was small, not especially strong and could not have moved the victim into the vehicle."

The investigators failed to produce the gun that Gwen used but the prosecution had another tool at its disposal.

The first link was Jim's watch that they found in Gwen's possession, which showed that she had tampered with the crime scene. The prosecution showed how she was going to use the money from the insurance policies and start a "home for troubled people" that would be near the spot where she killed her husband.

The jury found her guilty of first-degree murder and Hendricks was sentenced to life in prison.

"I just kept my faith that Jim would come rescue me and I would be set free from prison," Gwen said. "Of course, that never happened."

Inside the prison, physicians deemed her to be mentally unfit to be included with the general population and transferred her to the psychiatric unit.

"They got me on anti-psychotics," Gwen said. "And anti-depressants but it wasn't until 1997 that I started having memories of what had happened. At first, it was like just pictures and they hit me like bricks, you know. I killed a great husband and Dad. I robbed Season and Ben of their father. I felt lower than dirt."

She did have help, however, as some legal advocates filed briefs on her behalf, claiming that she had been insane at the time of her trial.

In September of 2000, the Supreme Court of Colorado overturned Gwen's conviction and ordered a new trial.

In April of 2001, a judge ruled that Gwen was not guilty by reason of insanity.

The trial lasted ten minutes.

"She came to terms with what she had done," Smith said. "She had stopped protesting, stop denying and admitted to what she had done."

Gwen was then remanded to a psychiatric care facility in Colorado. She then decided to change her name to "Emi Masai".

"When I lost Jim," Gwen said. "I also lost my children. I longed to be a wife and mother again. I redefined myself as married to Christ and being a mother to all the people I meet."

"By renaming herself she thought that she could obtain a new identity," Smith said. "It was a way of divorcing herself from her past transgressions."

Gwen went through four years of psychiatric treatment where the physicians determined that she was no longer a threat to society. She was released to a residential program where she now helps the needy at Mercy Ministries.

She continues to take her anti-psychotic medication.

"I never want to slip back into mental illness again," Gwen said. "I literally thank God every morning I open my medicine cabinet. I've always said justice wasn't done. Justice in this case would have been my execution. A life for a life. But it's not about fairness. It's about recognizing mental illness and knowing that you're not responsible for what you are doing when you're psychotic."

Gwen has had minimal contact with both her son and step-daughter since she committed the murder of their father.

"I long to see them but they let it be known through family channels that they don't want to see me," Gwen said. "So I respect that."

"I'm really glad that Gwen has helped herself enough to admit what she's done," Season said. "And I hope there never is a time where it gets easy for her to look in the mirror. Because there's never a time where it's easy to be without our Dad."

"I wish I could take it back," Gwen said. "Be a good wife and Mom again. I can't turn the clock back. So all I can do is give them my deepest apology and ask them to forgive me."

SERIAL KILLER JUANA BARRAZA

MARCUS MOORE

Juana Barraza is perhaps the most famous serial killer in all of Mexico's history. Authorities have attributed the death of up to 48 elderly women in Mexico to Juana, and she was found guilty in 2008 of several murders and was sentenced to a total of 759 years in jail for her crimes. Referred to as Mataviejitas, or Little Old Lady Killer, Juana's killing spree and the subsequent police investigation, became national news in Mexico in 2007 and 2008, and led to widespread pressure on the police department to solve the series of crimes against the nation's most vulnerable members of society.

Background

Juana Barraza, or Juana Dayanara Barraza Samperio, was born on December 27, 1958 in the small rural town of Epazoyucan, Hidalgo, located north of the nation's capital of Mexico City. Her father, Trinidad Barraza, was a local police officer and her mother, Justa Samperio, was a prostitute. Juana's mother left her father shortly after Juana's birth to begin a relationship with a married man named Refugio Samperio, was was Justa's stepfather during her childhood.

Juana reportedly suffered from a difficult and violent childhood, living with an extreme alcoholic for a mother. She was illiterate as a child and was often physically and emotionally neglected by her mother. She would later claim that her mother sold her to a strange man named Jose Lugo when she was only twelve years old for just three beers; the man sexually assaulted Juana repeatedly and she became pregnant with a boy. Juana would eventually have a total of four children, although her oldest son died in a robbery attempt at 24 years old.

Prior to becoming famous for her role as a serial killer, Juana was a relatively little-known wrestler who participated in the amateur circuits of *lucha libre*, a famous form of Mexican wrestling that involves the use of masks and significant amounts of stage drama. During her career as a wrestler, she performed under the stage name *La Dama del Silencio*, also known as The Silent Lady in Spanish.

While Juana toured the country as a part of the amateur wrestling circuit in the 1980s and 1990s, she turned to stealing and burglary in 1995 after birthing her fourth child. In 1996, she began robbing elderly people with a friend of hers, setting up a pattern of targeting the elderly that would last throughout her entire criminal career. The two burglars would dress in all-white scrubs and pretend to be nurses in order to gain their victim's trust and access to their homes.

Crimes

Juana's profile as a serial killer was that she consistently targeted elderly women, in their late 60s or older. Many of her victims lived alone and had little contact with local relatives or a strong social circle. Juana would typically befriend the victim, then lure them to their home or a quiet place where she would bludgeon them to death with a heavy object or strangle them with an extension cord that she carried on her person, usually robbing the victim once they were dead.

Juana used several different methods to gain her victims' trust. She would often cruise the streets of poorer neighborhoods, looking for elderly woman who were by themselves and struggling with bags of groceries or other household items. She would then offer to help the elderly women up their set of stairs to their apartments, where she would the kill her victim. Juana would also frequently pose as a government official, complete with an ID badge and government application forms. She would claim that she was going door-to-door to help pensioners apply for their benefits in order to gain their trust and access to their home. She frequently used phone cords, extension cables, tights, or a stethoscope to strangle her victims.

It is suspected that Juana's first victim was Maria de la Luz Gonzalez Anaya, who was murdered on November 25, 2002. Juana gained access to her apartment, likely in order to rob the elderly woman, but ended up killing Maria Gonzalez after the woman made disparaging comments about Juana, angering her and leading to her strangling the victim in a fit of rage.

Several years into her career as a serial killer, Juana Barraza began a romantic relationship with Jose Francisco Torres Herrera, a taxi driver known as *El Frijol*, or The Bean. Together, the two continued her killing spree and began by targeting Carmen Camila Gonzalez Miguel, an 82-year old wealthy woman in Mexico City. While the pair did successfully kill Carmen and escape, this murder led to a widespread police response and investigation into the existence of a serial killer in Mexico City. Carmen Gonzalez was the mother of Luis Rafael Moreno Gonzalez, a well-known and powerful criminologist. Her death led to increased police patrols, a public information campaign, and a collaboration with French investigators, who had recently detained *The Monster of Montmartre*, a prominent French serial killer.

Police Investigation

During the early stages of the investigation into a potential serial killer, the chief prosecutor for Mexico City, Bernardo Batiz, publicly said that he thought the killer had "a brilliant mind, quite clever and careful" and that he suspected the killer was adept at gaining the trust of their potential victims prior to killing them. Several officials believed that the killer was posing as a government benefits counselor who established trust by offering to help the victim secure government benefits like health care and welfare.

There was an odd coincidence which confused the police working on the case and led to detectives investigating misleading information that ultimately delayed Juana's capture. Early on, the police noticed that at least three of the women killed by Juana owned a copy of the *Boy in Red Waistcoat*, a famous painting from the 1700s by French painter Jean-Baptiste Greuze. For some time, police were convinced that the presence of this painting had some important bearing on the case and why the victims were chosen; but, ultimately it became clear that the presence of the painting was mere coincidence and that the police department's focus on this "evidence" was misplaced.

Police were able to determine through their investigation and subsequent in-person interviews that Juana was clinically classified as a psychopath: she did not feel any pain or remorse for actions, and thus had no moral qualms about her actions and their effects. Psychologists say that Juana associated the elderly women that she preyed on with her mother, believing that her actions were a net good because she was removing evil people from the world. Her lack of empathy, combined with her engaging persona and false identity as a government worker, allowed her to gain these women's trust in a small amount of time.

Despite the rash of killings in Mexico City in late 2005 and early 2006, the local police department consistently dismissed any theories of an emerging serial killer and called out such ideas as "media sensationalism." However, police did begin to take reports of a serial killer seriously in November 2005, when they received several witness statements reporting that the killer wore women's clothing, leading them to suspect that the serial killer was actually a transvestite who posed as a woman to gain access to, and trust from, his victims. On one particular occasion, the killer was seen living a victim's house wearing a red blouse.

Once the police department finally did launch a full investigation of the killings, their first action was to launch a city-wide raid of all of the areas frequented by transvestite prostitutes, since they mistakenly believed at that time that the killer was a transvestite who dressed as a female in order to gain the trust of his female victims. A reporter for La Jornada, a popular newspaper in Mexico City, would call the series of raids "ham-fisted" unproductive.

In addition to detaining and questioning all of the city's known transvestite prostitutes, the police also began visiting the local morgue to check fingerprints. They believed that the killer may have committed suicide and that they need only verify the identity of one of the corpses to close the case. This belief would quickly prove to be incorrect.

Despite initial fumbling by the police department and an investigation predicated based upon incorrect assumptions about the killer, the case would soon break open in a very public way. On January 25th, 2006, a suspect was seen fleeing from the home of the now-deceased Ana Maria de los Reyes Alfaro, an 82-year old women living in the Venustiano Carranza section of Mexico City. Ana Alfaro was strangled to death with a stethoscope by Juana Barraza. Luckily for the police, Alfaro was a landlady and one of her new tenants was arriving at her home as Juana attempted to flee the scene of the crime. The tenant nearly bumped into Juana as she rushed out of the building and was the first to see Reyes Alfaro's body. He immediately called the police and was able to provide the description that led to Juana's capture.

In a surprise to both the police, national media, and public, the suspected killer was actually Juana Barraza, a 48 year old amateur wrestler, and a woman that many people would mistake for a kindly grandmother; here was the famed Mexico City serial killer, and the nation was shocked.

Police investigators were initially drawn to the idea of a transvestite serial killer because of composite sketches and witness statements that described the serial killer as a masculine-looking woman. Given these statements and the fact that the vast majority of serial killers are men, they police department completely ignored the possibility that the killer could actually be a "masculine-looking woman," as opposed to a man dressed as a woman.

Despite this initial confusion, police quickly realized that Juana looked remarkably similar to the police sketches that had been composed from witness statements. The more that police learned about Juana, the more that her role as the serial killer made sense. Police initially thought that the killer had to be a man or male transvestite because of the sheer amount of strength required to strangle someone. They thought that it was impossible for a woman possess that much physical strength; however, Juana was no ordinary woman. She was a professional wrestler reportedly capable of bench pressing 200 lbs for multiple sets of ten, a significant sign of strength in any person.

Furthermore, her use of the stethoscope to kill her last victim was in line with witness statements, which had described a government worker with short, dyed-blonde hair and a mole on their face, carrying a stethoscope, benefit forms, and a government ID card.

Once detained, police were quickly able to connect Juana to at least ten other murders using her fingerprints. Mexico City's chief prosecutor at the time, Bernardo Batiz, would tell the media that "Fingerprints match in 10 murder cases, as well as one attempt." In addition, police investigators found several trophies related to the killings in her home, including cutouts of newspaper articles discussing the killings (despite the fact that she is illiterate). Juana admitted to killing Ana Alfaro, but said that she had initially visited the elderly woman's home in order to secure work during laundry and that she killed the woman out of "anger," and not because of any premeditated reason.

Trial

Juana Barraza began her trial for murder in spring 2008, with prosecutors claiming that she was responsible for up to 40 killings over the previous six years. While Juana admitted to killing Ana Alfaro, claiming that she murdered the elderly woman out of anger because she resembled Juana's abusive mother, she claimed that she was innocent of all of the other charges levied against her.

Despite her claims of innocence, Juana was sentenced to prison for 759 years in March 2008, after being found guilty of 11 separate murder charges and an aggravated burglary charge. Given that federal sentences in Mexico are served concurrently and legally the maximum sentence a person can receive is 60 years, it is likely that Juana will die in prison. However, she will be eligible for parole in 2058, when she is 100 years old.

Suspected Victims
Robbery
1995-2001
Juana is suspected of robbing a large, unknown amount of victims during this time period.
Murder
2002
November 24th: Maria de la Luz Gonzalez Anaya (64 years old)
2003
March 2nd: Guillermina Leon Oropeza (84 years old)
July 25th: Maria Guadalupe Aguilar Cortina (86 years old)
October 9th: Maria Duadalupe de la Vega Morales (87 years old)
October 24th: Maria del Carmen Munoz Cote de Galvan (78 years old)
2004
February 20th: Alicia Gonzalez Castillo (75 years old)
February 25th: Andrea Tecante Carreto (74 years old)
March 20th: Carmen Cardona Rodea (76 years old)
March 26th: Socorro Enedina Martinez Pajares (82 years old)
May 24th: Guadalupe Gonzalez Sanchez (74 years old)
June 25th: Esthela Cantoral Trejo (85 years old)
July 1st: Delfina Gonzalez Castillo (92 years old)
July 3rd: Maria Virginia Xelhuatzi Tizapan (84 years old)
July 19th: Maria de los Angeles Cortes Reynoso (84 years old)
August 31st: Margarita Martell Vazquez (72 years old)
September 29th: Simona Bedolla Ayala (79 years old)
October 24th: Maria Dolores Martinez Benavides (70 years old)
November 9th: Margarita Arredondo Rodriguez (83 years old)
November 17th: Maria Imelda Estrada Perez (76 years old)
2005
January 11th: Julia Vera Duplan (60 years old)
February 10th: Maria Elena Mendoza Vallares (59 years old)

April 13th: Maria Elisa Perez Moreno (76 years old)

April 14th: Arturo Patino Barranco (74 years old)

April 19th: Carolina Robledo (79 years old)

April 20th: Ana Maria Velazquez Diaz (62 years old)

June 17th: Celia Villaliz Morales (78 years old)

June 29th: Maria Guadalupe Nunez Almanza (78 years old)

July 5th: Julia Vargas (64 years old)

July 5th: Mario Cruz Flores (84 years old)

July 20th: Emma Armenta Aguayo (80 years old)

August 9th: Emma Reyes Pena (72 years old)

August 11th: Carmen Sanchez Serrano (76 years old)

August 15th: Dolores Concepcion Silva Calva (91 years old)

September 28th: Maria del Carmen Camila Gonzalez Miguel (82
years old)

September 28th: Guadalupe Oliver Contreras (85 years old)

October 18th: Maria de los Angeles Repper Hernandez (92 years
old)

2006

January 25th: Ana Maria de los Reyes Alfaro (84 years old)

Juana' Public Response

Juana has repeatedly denied that she is a serial killer, although she
has admitted to at least one murder. During her first appearance in
court for her trial, she stated "I only killed one little old lady. Not the
others. It isn't right to pin the others on me." When she was later asked
about her motive for the sole killing that she took responsibility for, she
simply said, "I got angry."

Juana has maintained her innocence throughout her trial, verdict
and during her current stay in prison, remarking at her verdict, "May
God forgive you and not forget me." She has vowed to appeal all but
one of the charges she was found guilty of, claiming that her sole killing
was a crime of passion against Ana Alfaro on the day she was caught.

TWISTED SISTERS : THE TRUE STORY OF REGINA AND
MARGARET DEFRANCISCO

CHAPTER ONE

Regina and Margaret DeFrancisco are two sisters convicted of first degree murder.

On paper, the two sisters look like two girls you would see at a church social.

In school, both were good but not great students. Margaret was the pretty one. She would get all of the attention from the boys but return little interest.

Margaret was a student at Jones College Prep School, a selective public institution that is considered one of the top high schools in Illinois.

A little on the shy side, Margaret had a quick wit and sense of humor. Sweet-looking and pretty, she had avoided any kind of trouble throughout her young life. Her early photos suggest, however, that her subtle smirk was a couldn't contain the narcissism that was growing within.

"You would look at Margaret and see right through her," one of her neighbors said. "It was black, like was nothing there. She didn't seem like she had depth, like she had compassion."

Regina had a love for animals, particularly ponies. She rode horses and in her words, "never lost a show."

Regina was also the more extroverted of the two, wearing her emotions on her sleeve. She could mouth off and had a chip on her shoulder. She also had a thing for 'bad boys', seeing them as a reflection of herself.

"A lot of girls get turned on by the 'thug life'," forensic psychologist Marnie Clark said. "The DeFrancisco sisters definitely fit that mold. They were not out to play Mrs. Cleaver when they grew up. They were attracted to the gang lifestyle. They thought the drama was exciting."

The girls were raised by a single parent, Nora DeFrancisco. Nora raised the two sisters and their brother Joey in the Pilsen neighborhood of Chicago. Their father, Augie DeFrancisco was a small-time burglar and convicted drug dealer who had no involvement in the girl's childhood years. Their maternal grandfather, Gilbert Smith, was a former Chicago cop who was fired from the force in 1960 after admitting that he was "friendly with certain burglars."

Growing up in Pilsen, however, the girls could not avoid rubbing shoulders with gang members. They became enamored with gang culture, learning who fought against who and what the names of the gangs were. There were the Latin Counts, Kool Gang, Villa Lobos, Bishops, among many other offshoots. The girls knew what streets signified what gang members' territory and memorized their hand signals.

"Chicago is simply rife with gangs," Clark said. "It is inescapable, even to those in the more affluent communities. There is still a choice, however. For whatever reason, the DeFrancisco sisters were drawn to the 'thug life'. To a young person, it looks 'cool'.

They are the classic examples of young women who could not see the big picture and thought the thug life was something worth aspiring to."

The two sisters, with their striking brunette looks, could not help but come into the cross hairs of the local gang members. They began wearing dark lipstick and teasing their hair out. Margaret would get a tattoo on her belly. Regina would have the letter "R" tattooed on her leg as well as a drawing of a heart just above her breast. They would hang out on street corners and in front of the local liquor store, chatting up the neighborhood 'gangstas'.

"The changes in their make-up and dress signified the changes in their personality," Clark said. "They grew bored during their time at prep school. Even ashamed. They did not want to see themselves as nerds and hated that aspect of themselves. Starting in eighth grade, it was time to start rebelling. By the time they reached high-school, the thug life was part of their persona. Dark make-up. Tattoos. Hanging out with gang bangers. Alcohol and drugs. But most important, they wanted all the drama that came with that kind of life. Who is out to get who, who dissed who and who shot who became their modus operandi in life."

Grandfather Gilbert, however, had seen this all before as a Chicago cop. He feared that the girls, particularly Regina, would become ensnared by the street gang culture. He tried to obstruct this from happening and found Regina a job with a local periodontist. He figured if he kept the girl busy with school and work it would keep her away from the idiots on the street.

Regina, however, did not have the emotional maturity to see the light. She showed up late for her first couple of shifts then she was fired.

But she had started dating a man named Johnny Rivera, a known member of Chicago's notorious "Latin Kings" street gang. Rivera had a rap sheet as long as "War and Peace" as well as more aliases than a Russian spy

Regina would learn how to package and deal drugs at the foot of Johnny. She would watch him put the cocaine into plastic bags, measuring it out by the ounce. They would drive around town and Johnny would introduce her to his customers, watching as he conducted the deals. The secret handshakes and secret lingo all became apart of Regina's world.

Officially crossing over from innocent prep school girl to drug dealing girlfriend, Regina lived a double life. She did manage to get a part-time job doing data entry work for a local law firm and had enrolled in the local junior college (Harold Washington).

Margaret was getting into trouble as well. Her grades in high school were slipping as she would sneak out at night to be with friends. She would often come to school looking "disheveled" according to one teacher who thought she looked like a child whose parents were going through a divorce.

And there was trouble on the home front.

Neighbors would report hearing the girls fighting with their mother on a daily basis.. The two girls were out of control with no father figure to put them in line. Nora would berate Regina whenever she would act up in school or get arrested and the girls would yell back.

In private, Nora would refer to her daughters as "the bitches".

Things would come to a head when Regina would get arrested for selling cocaine to an undercover cop. A single mom already strapped for cash as she had to support three children on her own, Nora was livid as she paid Regina's bail.

"How are you going to pay me back?" .

"I don't know!"

"Do you know how much it costs to bail you out of jail!" Nora screamed. "You are going to pay me back. You're going to pay me back every penny!"

CHAPTER TWO

"She needs money," Margaret said, her voice full of concern.

"How much?" Oscar asked.

"One thousand dollars. Can you help us out, baby?"

That was the scene set for the twenty-two year old Oscar Velazquez in June of 2000 as he spoke to the sister of his current teenage crush, Regina DeFrancisco. He spotted Regina around the neighborhood of Pilsen and quickly fell for her dark Irish-Italian good looks. Showing off his brand new Z28 Camaro, he chatted up the girls before he asked Regina out for tacos. The two began going out but Regina didn't like him...at first. Then she realized that he had some money and was all too willing to spend it on her.

"Oscar wasn't the typical guy that Regina would go for," Clark said. "Regina liked the 'bad boy', the thug. Oscar wasn't in street gang culture. He had immigrated from Mexico and actually had a real job, earning his living the old fashioned way as a truck driver. If anything, Regina would see someone like him as a sucker, someone who she could use."

Still, Regina was what Oscar wanted. He persisted in calling her, asking when he could see her again.

"He's a creepy guy," Regina told her sister, Margaret as her cell phone rang. She looked at the caller ID. Yep, it was Oscar.

"But maybe you can get some money from him?"

"Here, you talk to him," Regina said handing the cell phone to Margaret. "Just make up some baloney that I'm in jail or something."

"What?"

"Get rid of him. Tell him I need bail money."

"Hello, Oscar?" Margaret answered the phone.

"Yeah," Oscar said. "Who is this?"

"It's Margaret," she said, sounding as if she was trying to stifle tears. "Regina is in jail. She's locked up."

"What?"

"They put her in jail for something she didn't even do. They want one thousand dollars. One thousand dollars to bail her out."

Margaret smiled like a devil at her sister.

"I can help," Oscar said.

"No," Margaret said, sniffling. "It's too much."

"It's for your sister."

Oscar would persist in his willingness to help out, however. Margaret played him like a violin, agreeing to meet with Oscar to take his hard earned money.

"Oscar gave Margaret the money in the hopes of scoring points with the sisters," Clark said. "He thought that by being 'nice' and bailing them out of trouble they would find him attractive. Instead, it just fueled their contempt for him. These girls liked thugs. Bums. They cared little for Oscar's chivalry."

Regina would not use the money to pay back her mother, however. She would give the money to her real boyfriend, Johnny, who bought an "old school ride" car with Oscar's money.

Oscar would call Regina over twenty-four times during the next five days wanting to know what happened. He began to feel like the sucker he was.

He had a wife and kids in Mexico. But here in Chicago he fell for the brown-haired beauty and became all too willing to be her patsy.

"Oscar was playing with fire," Clark said. "He just didn't realize how far gone the girls were in terms of narcissism. He didn't see the fact that they didn't even see him as a human being. All he saw was batting eyelashes and pretty faces. He was totally smitten with Regina despite the fact that he had a wife and kids back in Mexico. Here he was, in Chicago, where he was free from the responsibilities of family. He could have a little fun and if he had to spend some money to do it, so be it."

CHAPTER THREE

The two sisters were surprised at how easy it was to extract money out of Oscar. With one fake phone call, they had one thousand dollars cash to their name.

"They were both attractive girls in the neighborhood," Clark said. "They were young, looking up to gang members and drug dealers for the power they had. But the girls realized that they had their own power. The power of budding sexuality that could make men do what they wanted. They could trick men into doing things for them with a future promise of sex."

Oscar continued to call and it would be only a matter of time before he would be confronted with the truth that he had been lied to. The girls had to construct a plan to get rid of him.

"I have an idea," Margaret said, picking up the cell phone and calling their fifteen year old friend, Veronica Garcia.

"Need your help," Margaret said as Veronica picked up.

"For what?" Veronica asked.

"I need a gun. Can you get a gun?"

"A gun?"

"Can your boyfriend get a gun?"

Veronica, like the DeFrancisco sisters, was enamored with street gang members. She had a boyfriend who could obtain whatever you needed, drugs or guns.

"Why?"

"We're going to stick up and rob Oscar," she said.

"You're not going to kill him are you?"

"We're just going to scare him a little," Margaret laughed.

Veronica did as she was asked, getting a gun from her boyfriend and heading straight over to the DeFrancisco sister's home.

"Nice," Margaret said, looking the pistol over, closing one eye as she looked through the cross hairs. "So where we going to do this?"

"Right here," Regina said, waving her hands around the living room.

"No way," Margaret said. "If the neighbors complain about us screaming and yelling then they're going to hear a gunshot. Duh."

Regina looked around the home. The basement door caught her eye.

"We'll lead him down there," Regina said, leading her sister down the basement steps. "Nobody can hear anything down here. The noise will be drowned out."

"Here," Margaret said, removing some blue tarp from the shelf. She spread the material down on the basement floor in front of the steps. "We can't leave any blood stains."

"Check you out," Regina laughed. "Miss Perry Mason."

Margaret laughed as she flattened out the tarp, placing it in a perfect line with the basement stairs. "Okay," she said, walking halfway up the steps. "So if we shoot him from here," pointing her forefinger into a gun. "He'll fall straight down there."

"Perfect."

The two sisters giggled and gave each other fist bump.

"Here is where the disconnect took place," Clark said. "They had embraced an environment and a culture where there were a lot of faux tough guys. Guys who said they would commit violence but for the most part it was all talk. The girls took it literally. At no point did they realize the gravity of what they were doing. They wanted to be 'gangstas', they wanted to be seen as 'hard'. They didn't have the maturity or the experience to realize that all of those 'gangstas' that they look up to are in jail. They didn't see Oscar at all. He was less than human. Something that is used, discarded and desecrated when it is no longer of use."

CHAPTER FOUR

Oscar was surprised that Regina finally called him back.

"Hey," she said, her teenaged voice soft and inviting.

"You're out of jail?" he asked.

"Yeah," she said. "I really appreciate what you did for me. That was really sweet of you."

"No worries," he said. "I need my money back. Been calling you like crazy."

"I'm sorry, I've just been busy."

"Yeah, I understand. But I need my money back."

"I was wondering if there was some other way I can pay you back?" she said in a sensual tone of voice.

"Like?"

"Like, I know you think my sister is hot, right?"

"What's that got to do with anything?"

"It is something we've been thinking about," she said. "But if you're not cool with it, it's okay."

"Not cool with what?"

"We were wondering if," Regina giggled. "If you can come over for a threesome."

Oscar couldn't believe his luck. He had heard of white girls being freaky, he just didn't think he would ever be able to experience it himself.

Naive to their plan, he rushed over and parked his car outside their mother's home in the South Side of Chicago.

He knocked on the door and was greeted by Margaret and Veronica Garcia, a friend of the two sisters. He didn't see the .38 caliber semi-automatic pistol had in her back waistband.

"Does anyone else know you're coming over?" Margaret asked.

"No," Oscar mumbled, shrugging his shoulder.

Margaret nodded her head and let the young man in. He saw Regina step into the room holding a bin of dirty laundry.

An awkward silence ensued followed by even more awkward smiles. The two sisters fed off each others willingness to go through with the plan. Even if one of them had second thoughts, they would be deemed "soft" by the other.

They had to go through with the murder.

Both women looked over at the young man with come hither looks. Regina said nothing as she opened the basement door and walked down.

"You go with Regina," Margaret said smiling.

"Right," Oscar said, his heart pounding in anticipation as he followed her down.

Oscar heard Margaret's footsteps behind him. What he didn't know was that she had a gun pointed at the back of his head.

When he reached the bottom step, she pulled the trigger.

The young man died instantly, falling face first in the tarp.

"Holy shit!" Margaret said. "I had no idea it would be that fucking loud. It doesn't sound that loud on TV."

Margaret came down the stairs. She kicked Oscar in the head hard, sending more blood spraying across the floor and wall.

"Nobody heard," Regina said as she knelt down and began rifling through Oscar's pockets.

"What the fuck was that?" Veronica said, calling down from the top of the basement steps.

"Did you see that? " Margaret asked. "He fell down like a baby!"

The sisters took out his wallet which had over $600 cash. They took his cell phone then ripped off the sterling silver chain from his neck.

"What the fuck happened?" Veronica said, her voice trembling as she came down a few steps.

"We shot his ass," Margaret said. "He's dead. Look at that shit, he's bleeding through his ears."

"Why did you do it?" Veronica screamed. "Why? Oh my God!"

"Shut the fuck up!" Margaret screamed.

"Don't just stand there," Regina commanded. "Come and help."

Their lifelong friend could only watch as the two sisters took out his car keys and wrapped up his body in a flowery bed sheet.

CHAPTER FIVE

"The girls suffered from what I call the 'Lord of the Flies' syndrome," Clark said. "Here they are hanging out with drug dealers, obtaining guns, killing men in the basement. There is no parental figure in sight! They are left to fend for themselves and the end result is murder and mayhem."

With the dead body in the basement, both sisters peeked out their window, waiting for dark.

Confident that the entire neighborhood was asleep, they opened the door and carried Oscar's body out of the home.

The three girls struggled carrying the dead weight, wrapping his body with a comforter and the flowered bed sheet.

They opened up the trunk and placed the body inside.

"What are you guys doing?" a woman yelled from a window across the street.

The girls looked up startled.

"We're getting rid of some furniture" Regina called out. "No worries."

The girls waved at the neighbor as she moved away from the window.

"Nosy bitch," Regina whispered.

Margaret giggled. Veronica still scared, said nothing.

They got into the vehicle and drove to a vacant lot where they took out Oscar's body again.

"This is hard work," Regina complained. "Shit!"

They plopped the body on the ground, looking at it for a beat before Regina reached back into the trunk. She pulled out a bottle of nail polish remover and poured the liquid over the tarp.

"Are you sure that's gonna work?" Margaret asked.

"It says 'highly flammable'," Regina said, shrugging her shoulders.

Margaret lit a match and set the material on fire.

The flame went up immediately, the girls could feel the warmth on their faces in the cold Chicago night.

"Told you this shit would work!" Regina said.

Then as fast as the flame started, it quickly died down.

"Light another one," Regina said.

Margaret threw down another match, getting the flames going again as Regina doused the tarp with the remaining nail polish remover.

Satisfied, the girls quickly got back into the Camaro and drove off.

**

An anonymous call came into police headquarters reporting the fire in the vacant lot. The caller investigated further, however, and saw Oscar's arm sticking out through the fire. He called 911 again with a sense of urgency, telling them of the body.

CHAPTER SIX

When police on scene identified Oscar Velazquez' partially burned body, their initial knee-jerk reaction was that this was the work of a local street gang, a drug deal gone awry. But when they found the nail polish remover bottle, however, they quickly realized that this was the work of amateurs. A jealous girlfriend maybe.

Meanwhile, the DeFrancisco sisters cruised around town over the following days, trying to pawn off the Camaro.

"This is where the sisters make the guys in 'Dumb and Dumber' look like geniuses," Clark said. "They had only pre-planned the front end of the murder. Like most impulsive killers, they had no idea what to do after. Their greed took over and they decide to sell the Camaro. They have no papers for it, duh, and really can only sell a stolen vehicle to a thug. They find no takers as even the dumbest street gang member isn't going to buy a hot car from two teenaged girls. So they cruise around town and Oscar's brother spots them in the car."

The girls, failing in their sales efforts, would later abandon he vehicle behind a storefront and set it on fire.

**

The day after Oscar's killing, a mutual friend named Jessica Benitez stopped by the house. Jessica went downstairs and watched Margaret mop up a stain of blood near the basement steps.

"The hell is that?" she asked.

Margaret said nothing as she poured bleach over the blood, scrubbing hard.

"Dude bled all over the floor," Regina said. "But only after Margaret kicked him in the head. We called him over, told this idiot we'd have a threesome with him. Then we robbed his ass."

"But the blood stain on the floor-" Jessica asked, watching Margaret clean up.

"We killed a guy," Margaret said without remorse.

"He was going to kill us!" Regina said. "Margaret shot him in the back of the head. We searched his body and found a gun in his waistband. Then we wrapped him up in plastic and put him in his car."

"Holy shit, girl," Jessica.

"We're about to go on the run," Margaret announced.

"Aren't you scared?" Jessica asked, looking back down at the blood stain in the basement.

"I ain't scared of nothing," Margaret said. "You should have seen his head when I shot him. His brain oozed out like cheese."

Margaret made a rolling motion with her hands.

Jessica then accompanied Margaret to the store she purchased a bottle of blonde hair dye for her "disguise."

"We see here how the whole street gang culture has influenced the behavior of these girls," Clark said. "At any point in time, Veronica or Jessica could have went straight to the police. But they get caught up in the drama of the moment. The so-called 'loyalty' to their friend who, quite frankly, would shoot them up in a heartbeat if they knew that they were going to be a snitch."

Going off the tip from Oscar's brother, the police show up to question both Regina and Margaret. The duo denied ever seeing Oscar.

They then go to interview Veronica Garcia.

They found the jittery fifteen year old to be a different story, however. The teen quickly crumbled under the pressure of questioning and told the police the entire story.

Feeling the heat, the DeFrancisco sisters go on the run...

CHAPTER SEVEN

For all of their stupidity in committing the murder, the DeFrancisco sisters deftly avoided capture for almost two years.

They decided to split up. Margaret would go to live with their maternal aunt in Roscoe, Illinois, an hour and a half drive away from where they lived. Roscoe was a small town with less then 10,000 people, a far cry from the drug infested streets of Chicago. Margaret's worst dreams were now realized. She was now a nerd who had to stay inside all day long, living in a boring cul-de-sac with no street gang action. Neighbors would remark that they would never see her and if hey did she would quickly go back inside.

Living underground without detection, it took a broadcast of the television show AMERICA'S MOST WANTED to generate an anonymous tip which led to Margaret's whereabouts. Police staked out her aunt's apartment and entered, finding Margaret in her bedroom with a blank look on her face.

"My feelings were hurt bad because she (my wife) did something behind my back," Margaret's uncle by marriage said later. "I knew (police) were going to find her anyway."

Seven months later, Regina was captured in Dallas living with her Latin King boyfriend, Johnny Rivera.

Initially, she did not even know where the gang banger lived. She just knew the town, Laredo, and she journeyed there by bus. Regina would eventually find him, locating one of his relatives. She would live under an alias and claimed that she worked as a maid.

Police knew better. Regina made money by selling drugs under the Latin King banner.

Unlike Margaret, Regina had evaded the scrutiny of the America's Most Wanted viewers.

Her capture came about because she could not stop hanging out with the wrong crowd.

Two sheriffs were had mistakenly arrived at her boyfriend's apartment, wanting to serve a warrant to someone else.

Rivera allowed the deputies to enter his apartment but he had left a marijuana flake on his table. Police searched the apartment further and found several packages of crack cocaine ready to be sold.

The deputies arrested Rivera. They searched inside the apartment and interviewed Regina, who was groggy from a cocaine high. She showed them her false Texas identification and they let her go.

But the deputies smelled something fishy on her aside from marijuana. They had the apartment manager set up a meeting with her. She arrived at the complex in an SUV with another man. The police approached and the SUV sped away.

The high-speed chase down residential Dallas streets reached upwards of 90 mph. The SUV then slammed into a center median, the front tires blowing out.

Regina got out of the car and tried to sprint away. A deputy tackled her and they fell to the ground, her cell phone skidding across the gravel road. Sifting through her pockets, the officer found over $1,500 cash.

She was taken to Dallas County Jail where they discovered her true identity.

"We pulled her out of jail," said a Deputy Dodson. "I asked to see one of her tattoos, and she showed me...I called her by name, but she never said a word to me. She knew it was over."

She was then extradited to Illinois to stand trial for the murder of Oscar Velazquez.

CHAPTER EIGHT

The trial of the two women began in July of 2004 and both sisters pleaded not guilty by reason of self-defense.

But their friend, Veronica Garcia, had cut a deal with prosecutors in return for a lesser sentence. She would provide the testimony that would damn the two sisters to prison.

Garcia said that she didn't know what the sisters had planned. She had simply provided the gun to the DeFrancisco's which she thought would be used for a robbery only.

"I didn't see her shoot Oscar," Veronica said.

The prosecution brought forth additional witnesses in Jessica Benitez, Luciana Macias, and Maria Constantino, the neighbor.

"Both of them told me that they killed Oscar," Jessica said. "Margaret kicked him in the head so he could die faster."

"I saw them load the body into the back of the Camaro," Constantino said. "Regina told me that she planned out the killing."

Margaret, however, maintained their innocence. She said that Oscar came to the apartment angry because the sisters had tricked him out of one-thousand dollars.

"I shot him to protect Regina," Margaret said.

"Then why didn't you tell the reporting officer what happened?" the prosecution attorney asked.

"We would've got in trouble," Margaret said. "If I told the truth, I would've been there longer."

Regina DeFrancisco would also take the stand and claim self-defense as well.

"I came out of my bedroom," Regina said. "And he was there, cursing and screaming. He pulled a gun on me. I thought I was going to die. I curled up on the floor, in a fetal position. I begged for my life. Then I heard a gunshot and saw Margaret standing over Oscar, holding a gun."

"Whose idea was it to dispose of the body?"

"Veronica knew of this vacant lot," Regina said. "It was her idea."

The jury would deliberate for over six and a half hours. Regina would be found guilty of murder. Margaret's jury, however, was unable to convict her. There was and 11 to 1 deadlock with one juror believing that she should be acquitted. The juror did not believe that someone so young could commit murder.

Margaret was then released from custody and told to await retrial. She had a baby during this time, a girl, and would find work as a nursing assistant while she awaited another trial.

Four months later, Margaret would be given another day in court. Veronica Garcia would once again be the star witness for the prosecution, detailing the exact same testimony as before.

There would be no deadlock in this second go around as Margaret would be convicted of first-degree murder.

Regina would be sentenced to 35 years in prison while Margaret would be sentenced to 46 years. Both women are now jailed at the Dwight Correctional Center. They have each filed appeals which have been denied.

"The girls cared nothing about Oscar Velazquez," Clark said. "In the end, they remained true to their own narcissistic nature. They only cared about what was happening to the next. They cared about nothing about the now fatherless children Oscar Velazquez would leave behind nor about the fact that the took his life."

Veronica Garcia was jailed for five years. She served her full sentence and has since been released.

"This is a cautionary tale if there ever was one," Clark said. "The sisters had it all. They had access to one of the finest schools in their state. Yet they chose to throw it all away for short money and the cheap thrill of the 'thug life.' In the end, they got to see what the 'thug life' was really all about. Mindless violence where everyone is out for themselves, especially when there is a plea bargain to be made. They could have had it all had they stayed on the straight and narrow. Now they have nothing."